Canon
and
Community

Canon and Community

A Guide to Canonical Criticism

by
James A. Sanders

Wipf and Stock Publishers
150 West Broadway • Eugene OR 97401
2000

Canon and Community
A Guide to Canonical Criticism

By Sanders, James A.
Copyright© 1984 by Sanders, James A.

ISBN: 1-57910-434-7

Wipf and Stock Publishers 2000
150 West Broadway • Eugene OR 97401

Previously Published by Augsburg Fortress, 1984.

for Jim and Helen Elgin
Saints in Christ
Phil. 1:1

Contents

Editor's Foreword

Especially in recent years questions concerning the historical place and the theological significance of the canon have come to the fore in biblical criticism. On the one hand, there are new data and theories concerning the process which led to canons of scripture in Judaism and Christianity. On the other hand, some scholars—including the author of this volume—argue that attention to either the canonical process or to the final form of the canon can resolve many of the issues of meaning or authority left open by other—mainly historical-critical—approaches to the Bible. It is therefore altogether appropriate that this volume on canon and canonical criticism should appear in a series of books which introduce contemporary methods of biblical study.

But the treatment of problems and possibilities concerning the history and meaning of the canon is by no means new in biblical criticism. In fact, most introductions to the OT and NT have traditionally included, usually connected with discussion of text, treatment of the history and contents of the various canons. The basic question concerning canon is a simple one: Which books are included in the Bible? But when one reviews just the tables of contents of the scriptures in the various religious communities—Christian and Jewish—which hold the Bible dear, the answer is far from simple. It becomes even more complex as one raises the historical and theological question: Why these particular books and in this order, and not some other list? As Professor Sanders points out, addressing these questions is an essential point of departure in the study of the Bible.

Beyond treatment of these more-or-less traditional issues concerning the history and contents of the canon, Professor Sanders addresses questions concerning the relationship between critical biblical scholarship on the one hand, including literary and historical methods, and biblical theology and hermeneutics on the other. He addresses directly the problem of the relationship between the recovery of the ancient meanings of texts and their contemporary authority and significance. This he does in part by calling attention to the way questions of authority and truth were focused at each stage along the canonical process, and in part by showing that how biblical texts and books functioned in ancient communities of faith may serve as models for contemporary understanding, again in communities of faith.

Finally, Sanders attempts to say what is central and fundamental to the Bible as a whole—the canon—and what is not. It is a bold step, and one that doubtless will not go unchallenged. But such a step is central to what he understands canonical criticism to be, that critical scholars should also and in the process of critical work attempt to discern what is normative in the Bible and thus also decisive for the believing communities which mean to take the Bible seriously. The book is, then, in many ways a treatise on the ancient and modern meaning of the Bible.

Emory University   Gene M. Tucker
Atlanta, Georgia
Summer 1983

Acknowledgments

This book began in 1976 as the Currie Lectures at Austin Presbyterian Seminary in Austin, Texas. Preston Williams was president at the time. Friends there have been exceedingly patient with me in waiting for the printed version. They will perhaps see how my thinking has changed, and I hope improved, in the interval. Other lectureships have provided opportunities to test the ideas and reshape them: the Fondren Lectures at Southern Methodist University in 1975; the McFadin Lectures at Texas Christian University in 1979; the Crozier and Ayer Lectures at Colgate Rochester, also in 1979; and the Oreon E. Scott Lectures at Phillips University in 1981. They formed the basis of a two-day seminar in the *troisième cycle* of the doctoral program in biblical studies and early church history of the Universities of Fribourg, Lausanne and Genève, at Fribourg in 1981. The basic ideas were formed and reformed in innumerable walks in the Black Forest, summer after summer, with Père Dominique Barthélemy, my colleague in the United Bible Societies' Hebrew Old Testament Text Project (1969-1979).

My colleagues in the Ancient Biblical Manuscript Center at Claremont have been understanding of my desire and need to complete the manuscript despite the heavy responsibilities, shared with them, of building an institution from scratch: deep-felt expressions of gratitude for loyalty go to Mrs. Margaret Woodruff, Mr. Richard Weis, Dr. Marvin Sweeney, and Mr. Peter Pettit.

My student, Gary Wilson, has given invaluable assistance in keeping up with the bibliography in studies in canon. I want also to thank Nancy Bowen, Robert Hall, and Mrs. James Webb, for their dedication and unselfish gifts of time and labor.

Special thanks go to my student, Peter Pettit, for his scrupulous reading of the manuscript. His attention to every detail in it induced some reworking and reshaping and several significant improvements. My thanks also to Lynn Pettit who, with Peter, typed the draft sent to the publisher. And thanks to Auburn Theological Seminary in New York City for special assistance in making the completion of the manuscript possible.

xi

I want to thank my friends and colleagues, Gene M. Tucker, Norman A. Hjelm, and John A. Hollar, for their longsuffering patience in waiting over two years for the manuscript. When I became president of the Ancient Biblical Manuscript Center in the late fall of 1980 work on the book came to a complete halt and could not be resumed until the spring of 1983. Their understanding and encouragement kept the vision alive.

Dora Cargille Sanders, who reminds me betimes that I am only her first husband, is my constant support and steady reminder that life can be sheer fun.

It gives me great pleasure and satisfaction to dedicate this book to Jim and Helen Elgin. Jim and Helen have become family for Dora and me in our life on the West Coast. They are truly saints in Christ (Phil. 1:1). Jim is Chief Financial Officer on the Board of Trustees of the Ancient Biblical Manuscript Center. He and Helen caught the vision of its importance early on and have been its and my steady support. Jim is a poet and lay theologian and has become my close friend; they are the prospective readers I keep in mind when I write about the Bible as canon. Helen and Jim have given me renewed understanding of the incarnation faith. Communicants in the Pasadena Presbyterian Church where they were married forty-five years ago, they are a blessing to all they touch. May God continue, for many years to come, to give them the strength of faith they have given to so many others. God bless you, Jim and Helen.

Claremont, California　　　　　　　　　　　　　　JAMES A. SANDERS
September 16, 1983

Abbreviations

ANQ	*Andover Newton Quarterly*
B.C.E.	Before the Common Era
BTB	*Biblical Theology Bulletin*
CC	*Christian Century*
C.E.	The Common Era
HBT	*Horizons in Biblical Theology*
HTR	*Harvard Theological Review*
IDBSup	*Interpreter's Dictionary of the Bible,* Supplementary volume
Int	*Interpretation*
JAOS	*Journal of the American Oriental Society*
JBL	*Journal of Biblical Literature*
JBR	*Journal of Bible and Religion*
JR	*Journal of Religion*
LXX	Septuagint
MT	Massoretic Text
NT	New Testament
OT	Old Testament
SBL	Society of Biblical Literature
USQR	*Union Seminary Quarterly Review*

Prologue

Spirit and Community

I sometimes say to pastors' groups and lay audiences that I have good news: the NT is also biblical! There is generally laughter; then I go on to explain that while questions arose in the churches after Marcion, about 150 C.E., as to whether the OT was canonical, the question in the minds of the NT authors was something like the opposite. They were concerned to show, throughout the NT, that what they were convinced God had just done in Palestine, in Christ and the early church, was rooted in Scripture, what we call the OT. I go on then to say that while I have Jewish colleagues who debate the point, I am sure Christians would not.

Christianity has become so systemically Marcionite and anti-Semitic that only a truly radical revival of the concept of canon as applied to the Bible will, I think, counter it. This "Guide" is designed to report to fellow scholars, and to pastors and lay people, why and how canonical criticism arose, the needs it attempts to address, and how to go about understanding it and using it as a subdiscipline of biblical study, complementary and supplementary to those critical disciplines and tools which have been developed and refined since the Enlightenment.

Its focus is on the function of the Bible as canon in the believing communities which formed and shaped it and passed it on to their heirs of today. Canon *and* community. They go together. Neither truly exists without the other. Enlightenment scholarship subsequent to the Reformation has so focused on original, historical meanings that it has very nearly decanonized the Bible. Its proper *Sitz im Leben*, or life setting, is the believing communities, Jewish and Christian, which find their identities in it and try to live their lives in the light of it. Its proper life setting is not the scholar's study but the liturgical and instructional programs of believing communities; that is where it reaches full stature.

The movement of canonical criticism is that of a next, logical step in the development of biblical literary and historical criticism beyond form and redaction criticism. It moves beyond the last individual geniuses discernible in such study of the biblical texts into the ancient communities which made the crucial decisions about what the geniuses had said and done. Canonical criticism may perhaps be the corrective to what happened because of the Enlightenment, when the Bible was taken from the church lectern into the scholar's study. The movement of canonical criticism is that of the scholar's being openly willing to be a servant of the believing communities. Not those believing communities who are so frightened of Enlightenment study of these texts that they fire professors who dare to be honest, or worse perhaps, force them to be dishonest by making them sign doctrinal confessions. Canonical criticism is not for those believing communities. They have not taken the necessary prior steps; they have not demonstrated the depth of faith necessary to be "honest to God." They live by the fear that the faith will disappear if they allow honesty.

On the other hand, it is for those faithful who have discerned the hand of God in the Enlightenment just as the ancient biblical authors discerned the hand of God in the international Wisdom they learned from others. It may help those faithful to discern the immense power for truth the Bible conveys for a world living between the idolatrous pride of the Enlightenment and the debilitating fear of its most imposing result, the nuclear bomb.

Canonical criticism sponsors a rather radical revision of the model that has nearly always served for understanding the "inspiration of Scripture," with all its attendant problems, whether by conservatives or by liberals. The common and traditional model is that of inspiration from God or Holy Spirit to an individual in antiquity whose words were then more or less accurately preserved by disciples, students, schools, and scribes. The only difference between liberals and conservatives has been quantitative; for the one they were less well preserved, while for the other they were very well preserved.

Biblical criticism has tacitly subscribed to the model in its quest for original words and settings. Historical criticism has been primarily interested, until quite recently, in what was really said and done by the original biblical contributors, through the historian's interest in reconstructing original moments. Those textual passages which helped such reconstructions have been called genuine or primary, while later additions by editors or scribes have been called spurious or secondary. Rarely did the historical critic carefully delimit the exercise, with the result that generations of graduates of mainline seminaries have felt they could not preach on a "spurious" passage! The historian's exercise spilled over into the question of inspiration. Biblical criticism, perhaps unwittingly, has subscribed to the same model as fundamentalists and nearly all students of the Bible.

The model canonical criticism sponsors as more nearly true to what happened, and what happens, is that of the Holy Spirit at work all along the path of the canonical process: from original speaker, through what was understood by hearers; to what disciples believed was said; to how later editors reshaped the record, oral or written, of what was said; on down to modern hearings and understandings of the texts in current believing communities. It is not Jeremiah who is canonical; it is the Jeremiah books that are canonical. The Septuagint of Jeremiah, which is quite different in a number of ways from the Massoretic Book of Jeremiah which is translated in modern Bibles, was the sacred book of Jeremiah in the Christian churches for centuries. If one can understand that it was not the prophet Isaiah who was canonical, but the Isaiah book which is canonical, then modern reputable scholars would not need to insist that the sixty-six chapters stem from a single author.[1] Not even Jesus is canonical; at least, I have never heard of his being canonized. The gospels are canonical, and the epistles. Could not God in the Holy Spirit so work with all the individuals in the believing communities, at all the points along the way of canonical process, as to weave these texts to God's own purposes and truth? Without that same Holy Spirit continuing to work in the believing communities today, these texts cannot be the Word of God for them. The great theologians of the church have always insisted on that point. The Bible can be Word of God only as read or heard by living persons in communities of faith.

One might say that the "Integrity of Reality" reaches through the ancient struggles of our ancestors in the faith to monotheize, to pursue the oneness of God, over against all kinds of polytheisms and fragmentations of truth, seeking to touch the current believer and provide her and him with the energy of that struggle to strive today to pursue the Integrity of Reality over against modern kinds of polytheism. The promise is that some of that integrity might rub off on such a believer.

The model of the believing community understood in all that follows is that of a pilgrim folk en route through the ambiguities of present reality to the threshold of truth. This is the image of the elect in much of the Bible and especially in the Epistle to the Hebrews. We have perhaps lost this image of the church. Henry David Thoreau wrote, "We no longer camp as for a night but have settled down on earth and forgotten

---

1. Wm. S. LaSor, David A. Hubbard, and Frederic Wm. Bush, *Old Testament Survey* (Grand Rapids: Wm. B. Eerdmans, 1982), 365.

Heaven." Canonical criticism would revive the image, especially in use of the hermeneutic technique of dynamic analogy—attempting to hear the challenge of the prophets and Jesus by identifying with those they addressed. Those challenges bid us continue the pilgrimage in our own context which our biblical counterparts began.

Chapter I explains how canonical criticism arose and the needs it is designed to meet. Chapter II explains what is meant by canonical process and why the term is used to understand canonization. It stresses the function of authoritative traditions and texts, in ancient believing communities, on their way to becoming canon. Chapter III describes the hermeneutics used by biblical authors and tradents when they cited or alluded to authoritative traditions or texts. Chapter IV is programmatic and outlines some of the tasks canonical criticism needs yet to do. The epilogue then suggests how those same hermeneutics used by the biblical writers can be used, or slightly modified for use, in the believing communities today. It closes with a list of possible consequences if they do. An appendix explains the function and usefulness of the triangle as a tool in canonical criticism. It should be noted that I view this effort as a sequel and complement to *Torah and Canon* (1972).

I

Reasons Why

The subtitle of this little book may come as a surprise to some otherwise knowledgeable students of the Bible. Most scholars do not think of study of the Bible's formation as canon as a discipline in itself but think of canon as simply the final, mostly uninteresting, stage of a literary critical study of the Bible. Study of canon has become study of how the larger literary units, the several books, were received by the community at large as authoritative in a certain order or sequence. If much thought is given to the question at all, study of canon is seen as the final aspect of a literary critical history of the Bible's formation.

It was not always so. On the contrary, this attitude came about only after considerable struggle on the part of a few brave scholars in the seventeenth and especially the eighteenth centuries in their efforts to make the Bible fully available to Enlightenment methods of historical investigation.[1] Canon at that time for most people meant authoritative Scripture, and it was quite essential in effect for scholars to devalue the meaning of the word *canon* in order to apply to the Bible the developing tools of historical investigation borrowed from literary study in other fields. If one had lived then, one would certainly have wanted to be on the side of the new exciting efforts to see the Bible in its own historical contexts. Canon had meant the very authority of the existence of faith and practice of synagogue and church. There was the greatest reluctance to accede to the historian's apparent effort to sever the essential and existential relationship between Scripture and ongoing believing community. Conservatives perceived that such critical investigation of Scripture could not be retained in the scholar's study without effect in the believing community and the world at large.

We, at this point some 200 to 250 years later, have to appreciate the

1. See Johannes Semler, *Abhandlung von freier Untersuchung des Canons* (Gütersloh: Mohn, 1967). Brevard Childs (*Introduction to the Old Testament as Scripture* [Philadelphia: Fortress Press, 1979], 30–45) provides a short historical sketch of the resignification of the word *canon* in biblical criticism.

1

considerable apprehension of conservatives in this regard. Determination of the meaning of Scripture had always rested within the believing communities: it had been formed there and it belonged there, rather than in the historian's study. The Bible had always been the church's book and the Scripture of the synagogue, and it looked as though it was falling into foreign hands. This early apprehension actually still exists in some quarters.

But revival of a sense of canon in responsible biblical study does not mean reversion to a precritical view of canon. Literalists and fundamentalists can take only false comfort in what is happening in this regard: they should not be deceived into thinking that critical scholarship has come to its senses in repentance of its errant ways. Far from it. What is happening is an extension of biblical criticism as it has developed to date. Biblical criticism is evolving, so to speak, into its next phase. It is, in part, out of a desire not to deceive that some of us are calling this new phase canonical criticism, or canon criticism as some prefer. It has not yet fully developed perhaps into a discipline in itself, but there is little doubt that it will do so.[2] The main reason most of us who are engaged in it call the work canonical criticism is that the questions emerging require development of critical tools comparable to those which earlier evolved in historical-critical study of the Bible—textual criticism; source criticism; literary criticism; form criticism; tradition criticism; and, recently, redaction criticism.

Even Brevard Childs, who resists thinking of his own work on canon as a part of biblical criticism, must not be misunderstood as reverting to a precritical stance in Bible study. On the contrary, Childs uses all the valid tools of biblical criticism in his work and is developing methods for interjecting a canonical perspective in Bible study which simply cannot be seen in any light other than that of critical historical study of the formation of the text of the Bible as inherited through synagogue and church.[3]

An increasing number of students trained in the critical disciplines have expressed dissatisfaction with the implicit hermeneutics of the historical-critical method, but most of them have sponsored quite different hermeneutical moves as solutions. Hans Frei expresses the growing concern in perhaps the most responsible and generally acceptable way: the biblical story or narrative has become eclipsed by

---

2. *Pace* Joseph Fitzmyer "Judaic Studies and the Gospels: The Seminar," in *The Relationships Among the Gospels*, ed. Wm. O. Walker, Jr. (San Antonio: Trinity Univ. Press, 1978), 258.
3. See, for instance, Child's *The Book of Exodus: A Critical Theological Commentary* (Philadelphia: Westminster Press, 1974).

2

the work of the very scholars who know most about it.[4] One NT student calls biblical criticism bankrupt.[5] Quite a few thoughtful people, especially scholars in theological disciplines other than biblical, are putting it very simply: biblical criticism has locked the Bible into the past.

A critical reading of the Bible for the most part means recovering the points originally scored. That is the thrust of biblical criticism as it has developed since the Enlightenment. The attitude or posture of biblical criticism has been to devalue pursuit of the meanings the biblical text may have for the believing communities today. A serious put-down in critical circles is to call a treatise sermonic or homiletical. It means that the treatise is simply not to be taken seriously. The effect of the comment can be devastating to the student who wants credentials in the critical scholarly community, and for the most part the intention is to discourage. Sermons and homilies by definition seek meanings in the biblical text for believing communities today. But in scholarly circles the terms have become bywords used sometimes to ridicule, certainly to reject.

Biblical criticism started in the seventeenth and eighteenth centuries as a very exciting movement with great confidence that ancient biblical wisdom could be unlocked in new ways through Enlightenment methods and then wed with the new sciences to illumine divine revelation in ways never before dreamt of. It bore with it a new meaning of faith that could unleash intellectual honesty within the fold of traditional religious identity. The reader should clearly understand that, with very few exceptions, most biblical critics have been persons of faith, staying within a traditional believing community. All this has happened at home, so to speak. A few fundamentalists have perhaps attempted to read some biblical critics out of the household of faith, but they are not to be taken seriously. The actual number of biblical critics who have renounced their religious identity is very few indeed.

But, like most other movements, biblical criticism has produced problems as well as exciting results; those problems have to do with the effect of the exciting results in the believing communities. The value system of historical criticism is clear: the original meanings are the authentic ones, and only the tools of biblical criticism can recover those meanings. Hence one can now understand how it was necessary for biblical criticism to limit the concept of canon. And as biblical criticism

4. Hans Frei, *The Eclipse of Biblical Narrative* (New Haven, Conn.: Yale Univ. Press, 1974).
5. Walter Wink, *The Bible in Human Transformation: Toward a New Paradigm for Biblical Study* (Philadelphia: Fortress Press, 1973), 1.

proceeded on its exciting path, coming up with historical hypotheses one after another, contradiction of traditional interpretation seemed to become an integral part of criticism. Not only so, but the results seemed constantly to undermine traditional views of authority, particularly in the matters of authorship of biblical texts and biblical chronology. Clash after clash seemed to ensue.

Within advanced theological circles, however, the real crisis did not emerge fully into the open until the 1960s. The principal reason for this was that serious theologians were responding in their own ways to the challenges of the Enlightenment, so that far from being shocked by what was happening among their colleagues in biblical studies, they saw there a parallel development. Western European theologians, often in conversation with biblical scholars, developed two great syntheses in succession. The theological syntheses are referred to, for lack of better terms, as first, liberal and second, neo-orthodox. One is reluctant to use such labels for two movements which had within them so many diverse thrusts, but each had a discernible hermeneutic character: liberalism stressed God as creator of all the world and neo-orthodoxy stressed God as particular redeemer in and through Israel and Christ—neither to the exclusion of the other, of course.[6] Much, much more would need to be said if space allowed, but that is an admissible description. The point is that each synthesis guarded the believing communities, which harbored or at least tolerated biblical criticism within their ranks, from the brewing crisis. Liberalism was viewed as capable of adapting the humanism and optimism of the eighteenth and nineteenth centuries to basic, abiding Christian values; neo-orthodoxy was viewed as capable of adapting the despair, disillusionment and need of humanity following the First World War, and the existentialist mood of the age, to the basic reformationist gospel of Protestant tradition.

Protestantism, that Western breakaway branch of Christendom dating to the sixteenth century and stemming in part from the Renaissance and Enlightenment, was the battleground. Those believing communities which harbored or tolerated biblical criticism were precisely the so-called established denominations of Protestantism: North European Lutheran and Reformed churches, the Churches of England and Scotland and their daughters in the English-speaking world, and the mainline denominations of North America. Reform Judaism was born in the nineteenth century in Germany as an accommodation to the Enlightenment and from the start sponsored

6. James A. Sanders, "Biblical Criticism and the Bible as Canon," *USQR* 32 (1977): 157–65, esp. 157–59.

4

biblical criticism, but the rest of Judaism has strongly resisted application of its method to Torah. Roman Catholicism, apart from some French scholars, vigorously resisted biblical criticism until the famous encyclical of Pius XII, *Divino Afflante Spiritu* (1943). While there has been theological movement somewhat reflective of liberalism and neo-orthodoxy in both Jewish and Catholic thinking, it is Protestantism which was founded in part on the principle of *sola scriptura* where the battles have been most openly fought. If Scripture was the sole ground of faith for Protestants, what was biblical criticism doing to that faith, insisting on what was originally intended and meant by a given passage rather than on what it had come to mean?

Both liberalism and neo-orthodoxy provided theological syntheses which could incorporate the exciting results of biblical criticism; they seemingly co-opted them, as it were, and thus staved off the impending crisis. There were two further hermeneutic movements at play. The one was *evolutionary* in thrust, for liberalism was wed in part to the thinking which developed in the Enlightenment in this regard: history has a goal. Biblical eschatology, so pervasive in both Testaments, could be absorbed into such thinking and modified to quite a palatable degree. The other movement was a sort of *primitivism*: the earlier the more authentic. Go back as far as possible to recover the origins and the authoritative roots. If one could really get back to Moses himself and Jesus himself, one would come face to face with the genius (whether superimposed by God personally, according to the more conservative, or implanted by God at creation, according to the more liberal) which commanded authority in its own right; one could encounter, supposedly, the self-asseverating and self-authenticating truth which instigated and nurtured biblical thinking.

But neither liberalism nor neo-orthodoxy, in the sense that both have functioned as syntheses, now protects us from the crisis which is building. The charges assail at every hand. With all its excitement, biblical criticism has indeed tended to lock the Bible into the past. It has been so keen on recovering original meanings that it has effectively decanonized the Bible or severed if from the ongoing believing communities. To protest that it did not intend to do so is of little value. It has happened, and it has been largely responsible for the gulf that now obtains between pulpit and pew, between the critically trained pastor and the lay parish. For some the Bible has become a sort of archaeological tell which only experts can dig. Even well-trained pastors feel that only their professors can read the Bible "right." To be fair it should be stressed that a part of the reason the charge is being made is that those

5

experts do come up, time after time, with very exciting results. A scholar may often hear from lay people in the churches: "I have never heard the Bible explained in such an exciting and relevant manner. Why have we not heard this before?" Probably because the local pastor gave up expository preaching for topical. Biblical criticism can be rightly viewed as a blessing for the believing communities. On the contrary, it has caused so much of the Bible to come alive in three-dimensional relief that biblical criticism is rightly sponsored by the churches at least through support of seminary faculties. In theological parlance, it may rightly be viewed as a gift of God in due season. But like many good things it has created its own problems.

With the two great syntheses no longer here to shield biblical criticism from the charges now with increasing voice being leveled against it, what might be the resolution of the now open crisis? Most such solutions have come as hermeneutics imported to the Bible, such as Rudolf Bultmann's existentialist reading of the Gospels and Paul, or that of his students in the so-called New Quest for the historical Jesus by stressing the later Martin Heidegger's view of language as the home of human being—the language-event (*Sprachereigniss*) hermeneutic of Ernst Fuchs, Gerhard Ebeling, and James Robinson. Both of these were heirs of the hermeneutic of progressive evolution of the nineteenth century and the thinking of German Christian philosophers such as Friedrich Schleiermacher. Another line deriving perhaps from the same more or less Christian humanist source was Wolfhart Pannenberg's effort to work through a theology of world history which could read both biblical sacred history and world secular history in the same manner. Jürgen Moltmann pressed Pannenberg's case into a "theology of hope" wherein the future aspect of universal history was stressed and stated as God's future continually invading the human present. Moltmann thus recognized the eschatological aspect of biblical thought, which had been somewhat muted in the others. Running parallel to all this mainly liberal line of thought was the neo-orthodoxy of Karl Barth whose preunderstandings were an imposing neo-Reformationist dogmatic of the Word of God which operated in a Christocentric hermeneutic of redemption.

The possibility of a new synthesis seems quite remote. Since the 1960s numerous ways of reading the Bible have been offered and have drawn some adherents, but we cannot speak of any one of them as synthesis. Only a few need to be mentioned to see a pattern of attitude toward biblical criticism.

Since the turbulent 1960s one has seen a rather massive turning away from the Word to the Spirit as central focus for theologizing.[7] This is a common move in the history of Christianity. When the doctrine of the Word no longer has seemed to provide grist for theological mills the church has often turned to the doctrine of the Spirit, or focused on the doctrine of Creation (for natural theology). Ages of the Word give way to ages of the Spirit, and vice versa throughout church history: so neo-orthodoxy has given way to secular and sectarian theology in many guises. One of the moves here is that of turning inward to the individual's private story as ground for theologizing with a concomitant turning away from the Bible, and not just from biblical criticism; another is that of turning outward to nature and creation. The current emphasis on one's personal story illustrates the one and the stress on working out a secular theology illustrates the other. But both moves turn away from the Bible, each in one way or another pointing out the apparent negative results of biblical criticism, locking the Bible into the past, as reason for doing so. While only the so-called liberals seem to be attempting secular theologies, both liberals and conservatives are involved in the pneumatic turn. They both seek God in personal testimony of what has happened in their own individual stories. Each may still find the Bible useful for prooftexting, but both are equally critical of biblical criticism.

A move stemming from biblical form criticism but spurred by recent studies in secular literary criticism and anthropology, especially in France, is structuralism. It is also called the field of semiotics for which the final form, any final form, of a biblical text serves for analysis. It has built a kind of ethos of denigration of traditional biblical scholarship. It seems that if someone in this field does at some point digress into discussion of what the biblical text originally meant an apology is issued with even an expression of regret that it had seemed necessary.

Another interesting hermeneutic imported to the Bible in similar manner is called symbolism, which shares some ground with structuralism. The emphasis is largely on the reader's situation and condition and the universal power of symbols and metaphors which emerge from the biblical text, no matter the original intention of the biblical authors. Historical criticism, if used at all, is employed only reluctantly and apologetically.

Closely related and, in the view of some, a part of the above are the numerous efforts since the 1960s to import political hermeneutics to the

7. Ibid., 159.

Bible, especially Marxist modes of reading texts. Another is that of bringing modern psychological modes of reading texts to Bible study, especially in groups where parables are acted out in role playing.

Some of the above, especially those employing structuralist, political, and psychological hermeneutics, tend to be a bit imperialist, even singularist about what they are doing, as though to say that all the others are wrong, or at least woefully lacking. They tend to cancel each other out a bit in this regard. There is the tendency to say that all of life is political, or that all readings are psychologically oriented one way or another.

But interestingly enough, all of the above modes of importing hermeneutics to the Bible stemming from the 1960s denigrate biblical criticism and more or less radically devalue the efforts in historical criticism which have evolved over the past 250 years. There is clear value in each mode, but one is not at all sure how long some of these recent moves will last, or how widely they will be accepted.

Some of the challenges to biblical criticism have come from quite a different quarter altogether, called functionalism. This is, however, quite historically oriented and those working out of such a perspective critique biblical scholarship scrupulously and carefully. They are being heard quite clearly. Here are investigations into how the Bible has functioned both in the believing communities and in the culture at large, and how it might continue to function in modern cultures and situations. In doing so they seem constrained to point out that biblical criticism, for all its exciting and very valuable finds, has to some extent eclipsed biblical narrative.

While there are other moves afoot, this is fairly much the situation as it obtains in intelligent readings of the Bible today. What should not be overlooked is that most of them are still concerned to pursue the relevance of the Bible today and that all of them, with few exceptions, still seek authoritative value in it.[8]

Quite distinct from these but sharing some of the same concerns is the recent move to revive a broader sense of canon for understanding the Bible. When one reviews the history of·biblical criticism since its inception, there is a kind of logic of evolution at work. From the early interest in seeking out the various component sources that went into the Bible's literary makeup, through form-critical and tradition-critical work on yet smaller literary units and sources, to rhetorical criticism and redaction criticism—in effect moving on to interest in larger literary

8. For references, bibliographic data, and further evaluation, see n. 6 above.

units in their final stages of composition—one can actually see how the next step in *that* line of biblical study, the literary critical, would evolve into interest as to how the large literary units (whole biblical books or large sections of Scripture) finally came together into the several canons which we inherit from antiquity. Canonical criticism is much more than observations about the final shaping of the Bible, but one can see how it has evolved out of earlier interest and work of historical-critical nature.

Study of canon as the final stage in a literary critical history of the Bible's formation was a result of the reduction in concept of canon effected by early biblical criticism. The young field at that time sought elements in the final stage of that literary history amenable to its developing tools of investigation and to the questions the field needed to ask: and those elements were councils and lists recorded in the noncanonical literature of synagogue and church.

One of the finds of biblical criticism in the late eighteenth century was the scattered evidence of a rabbinic assembly that took place in Jabneh, or Jamnia, in Palestine before the end of the first century C.E. There was without doubt a gathering there of Pharisaic-rabbinic leaders after the fall of Jerusalem in 69–70 C.E. when it was no longer possible for them to carry on life as usual in the Holy City and when Rome forbade such assemblies there. And there is evidence that the surviving Jewish leadership asked of themselves and their traditions the crucial existential questions of sheer survival. The modes of survival sought and found in the years between the two Jewish revolts, that of 66–69 and that of 132–135, set the pattern for Jewish identity and existence for centuries to come. Judaism changed character rather significantly precisely in that period in the sense that the normal pluralism that had obtained in the postexilic and especially Hellenistic and Herodian periods was over.[9] Only one denomination survived with clear Jewish identity, the Pharisaic; and even it changed character significantly enough to adapt itself to the survival of all Judaism. Judaism showed at that time its tremendous powers of adaptability.[10] In order to adapt to the challenges of being almost totally now a diaspora religion, but a religion scattered in a one-world-power, Roman, context, Judaism narrowed itself quite effectively from being a multiple-denomination religion of considerable pluralism—its mode of response to the challenges of the quite pluralistic Hellenism which had obtained since the late fourth century B.C.E.—to

9. Michael E. Stone, *Scriptures, Sects and Visions* (Philadelphia: Fortress Press, 1980); George W. E. Nickelsburg, *Jewish Literature Between the Bible and the Mishnah* (Philadelphia: Fortress Press, 1981).
10. Jacob Neusner has written extensively in clarification of this point: see, e.g., *From Politics to Piety: The Emergence of Pharisaic Judaism* (Englewood Cliffs, N.J.: Prentice-Hall, 1973) and *First Century Judaism in Crisis* (Nashville: Abingdon Press, 1975).

9

being in effect a single-denomination official religion (*religio licita*) in the politically unified Roman Empire. Many Jews of denominations other than the Pharisaic perhaps "converted" or changed identity and became either Christian (the other Jewish denomination which survived 70 C.E. besides the very few Samaritans) or assimilated to the dominant Roman culture with its multiple choices of religious identities available. The Essenes, at Qumran and in the towns and villages, would be a case in point: some undoubtedly became Christian, some became Zealots, some would have become rabbinic Jews; and some would perhaps have assimilated into the dominant culture. But if they became Christian, they would have, with the Christians, become in effect non-Jews, since by 100 C.E. Christianity and surviving Judaism were quite distinct.

There were significant changes in Judaism and Christianity as a result of the crucial event of 70, the classical date of the fall of Jerusalem and the second destruction of the Temple. The destruction of the Jerusalem Mother Church was as significant for Christianity as the destruction of the Temple was for Judaism and Christianity.[11] Because the Petrine church of Jerusalem was so radically wiped out, Christianity became almost totally dissociated from *the land* and seemingly lost its moorings in that regard altogether.[12] Its break with (pre-70) early Judaism was apparently more radical than the discontinuity experienced in surviving rabbinic Judaism. An aspect of that break was in its "Old Testament" canon. Until well into the early second century the so-called OT was the Scripture of Christianity. After 70 some Christian writings, such as the letters of Paul and traditions about Christ, began to take on considerable authority as well.[13]

But another aspect of the break of church from synagogue was the fact that the churches did not benefit from the discussions which took place with regard to canon at Jamnia, or more accurately, what happened in Judaism with regard to canon as reflected in the discussions at Jamnia.[14] It is prudent to be careful in speaking of the assemblies at Jamnia between 70 and 100 C.E. since a recent review of the literary evidence concerning those meetings indicates that the early biblical critics since Johannes Salomo Semler had gone beyond what the evi-

11. A point well made by Dieter Georgi in *Die Geschichte der Kollekte des Paulus für Jerusalem* (Hamburg-Bergstadt: Reich, 1965), 30–51, 79–96.
12. W. D. Davies, *The Gospel and the Land* (Berkeley and Los Angeles: Univ. of California Press, 1974), 336–75.
13. Kurt Aland, *The Problem of the New Testament Canon* (Westminster: Canterbury, 1962); Ernest C. Colwell, *New or Old? The Christian Struggle with Change and Tradition* (Philadelphia: Westminster Press, 1970); Hans von Campenhausen, *The Formation of the Christian Bible* (Philadelphia: Fortress Press, 1972), esp. 103–63.
14. Albert C. Sundberg, Jr., *The Old Testament of the Early Church* (Cambridge, Mass.: Harvard Univ. Press, 1964).

10

dence indicates.[15] We especially should not speak of a Council of Jamnia as introductions to and handbooks on the OT still do. The early critics apparently read into the rabbinic evidence there is about Jamnia too much, in thinking of it in conciliar terms. An important aspect of canonical criticism is the necessary debriefing we must do about Jamnia and all such conciliar thinking about canon. The discussions at Jamnia could only reflect what was already happening in the believing communities. We must not think of Jamnia in later Western terms of ecumenical councils with delegated authority either from above, some hierarchy, or from below, such as synagogues sending elected delegates with authority to vote on what should be in or out of the canon. Our Western ways of thinking unfortunately got in the way to the extent that we attributed to Jamnia some great authority to make decisions for all synagogues for all time. It was not that way at all.

Nonetheless, because there was such a radical break between Christianity and Judaism, the churches did not benefit from what was happening in Judaism, well indeed reflected at Jamnia, but rather retained much of the literature of Jewish denominations other than the Pharisaic of the pre-70 period. Two quite different sorts of experiences characterize the two faiths in the crucial post-70 period: while rabbinic Judaism was closing ranks, shedding all its denominations save one and considerably restricting its canon, Christianity, on the other hand, was spreading out into the Roman-Hellenistic world, becoming pluralistic in itself and significantly keeping its canon open-ended.

Prior to 70, Judaism with its several denominations had had an open-ended canon. Pharisaic Judaism, even before 70, had begun a process of restriction and stabilization of text and canon. All Jews had the Torah and most had the Prophets. It was the third section of the canon, the Writings (Hagiographa), which was open-ended. And it was mainly the books in the Writings (Hebrew, *Ketubim*) which were discussed at Jamnia, though portions of Ezekiel presented problems to a number of Pharisees and others who were against any form of mysticism in the faith. Other denominations, however, such as the Essenes, so much like the Christians in certain crucial matters of religious thinking, had more books in their third section (*Ketubim*) than did the Pharisees. And the churches retained these in their OT. We today call them the Apocrypha or deutero-canonical writings and the so-called Pseudepigrapha. Western Christianity, until the Reformation, retained the Apocrypha, and Roman Catholicism still has these books as an integral part of its canon.

15. Jack P. Lewis, "What Do We Mean by Jabneh?" *JBR* 32 (1964): 125–32.

Eastern Christianity, the various forms of Orthodoxy in the Slavic countries and the Near East, also retained the so-called Pseudepigrapha. The Ethiopian Orthodox Church in Egypt and Ethiopia even to this day has apparently the largest OT canon of all.[16] By and large Christianity retained in its OTs what the more eschatologically oriented Jewish denominations (e.g., the Essenes) had used.

The evidence for this until the discovery of the Dead Sea Scrolls was in what those Eastern Christian communions passed down, generation after generation, in an unbroken tradition. Many of the OT books not in the smaller restricted rabbinic Jewish canon were preserved and available only in translation in the languages of the churches. Now with the Dead Sea Scrolls we have original-language Hebrew and Aramaic texts of some of these, a tremendous boon to reconstructing the literary history of these documents and texts closer in time to the supposed "originals."

Moreover, the Scrolls have also provided new perspectives on the question and phenomenon of canon, perspectives similar to and parallel with a vantage point provided by the Scrolls on the history of the text of the Hebrew Bible. While no copy of the book of Esther has been found in the Qumran library of the Essene sect (basic Dead Sea Scrolls), all the other books of the Jewish canon are represented in the library, some such as the Psalter, Isaiah, and Deuteronomy quite well represented with numerous copies. But there were also scrolls precisely of the works we call the Apocrypha and Pseudepigrapha, and some of these are in the same careful bookhand-type script as those we call canonical. Similarly, formal copies of works heretofore totally unknown but of the type of Jewish literature precisely familiar from late biblical and apocryphal works were also included in the library, apparently side by side with the canonical. While they included only the formal type of biblical commentary called *pesher*, of what rabbinic Judaism calls canonical books, this observation is not restrictive; on the contrary, there are relatively few *pesherim* preserved and those we do have, on passages in Isaiah, Hosea, Nahum, Habakkuk, Zephaniah, Micah, and a few psalms, were all regarded by the Qumran sect as "prophetic" in nature. The large Psalms Scroll from Qumran Cave 11 specifically states (col. 27) that David wrote all his "songs" in a spirit of prophecy. The genre *pesher* was apparently limited to the literature considered by tradition to be prophetic.

16. R. W. Cowley, "The Biblical Canon of the Ethiopian Orthodox Church Today," *Ostkirchlichen Studien* 23 (1974): 318–23; Sean P. Kealy, "The Canon: An African Contribution," *BTB* 9 (1979): 13–26.

The last manuscript cave discovered at Qumran was more responsible than any of the others, however, for instigating a considerable review of what canon meant at Qumran. Prior to the discovery of the scrolls it had been commonplace to recite a certain hypothesis as almost dogma in discussions of OT canon: the Pentateuch was closed by 400 B.C.E., the prophetic corpus by 200 B.C.E., and the Hagiographa at Jamnia before the end of the first century C.E. The evidence for the scheme was meagre, but it had become a convention in study of canon in a literary critical approach. The above observations about the scrolls and the question of canon had not yet been put in such a perspective until the discovery of Cave 11. In it a copy of the Psalter (11QPs^a), in formal style bookhand such as was most frequently used for canonical books, was discovered containing seven psalms not included in the Massoretic, or traditional, Psalter; in it even the later canonical psalms were sometimes in an order different from the Massoretic. This caused a review of other copies of Psalms at Qumran which yielded information that other Psalms scrolls, from Caves 4 and 11, as yet unpublished, were of a character similar to the large Psalms Scroll (11QPs^a). In fact, one of these (11QPs^b) appears to be a fragment copy of the Psalter with exactly the same content and order as 11QPs^a, indicating at least that the latter was not maverick, or an altogether unique, special edition. A scroll of psalms from Cave 4 (4QPs^f) in like manner has Massoretic and non-Massoretic psalms included side by side though the non-Massoretic psalms are not those in 11QPs^a. There are copies of other Psalters from Cave 11 which include non-Massoretic psalms as well. All this caused a review of the extent of the Psalter as referred to in other ancient literature.[17]

Also from Cave 11 has come the largest of all the Dead Sea Scrolls, the Temple Scroll.[18] Its editor, Yigael Yadin, sees it as having been "canonical" at Qumran; nay more, he thinks it was viewed at Qumran as having been as authoritative as the books of the Torah itself![19] It is clearly written in the style of Pentateuchal books, employing the same kinds of hermeneutics literary criticism indicates editors of the Pentateuch used in composing it. In fact if we speak of the fifth book of the Torah as Deuteronomy, following its Greek title in the Septuagint translation, we might well speak of the Temple Scroll as Tritonomy.[20] It

17. James A. Sanders, "Cave 11 Surprises and the Question of Canon," in *New Directions in Biblical Archaeology*, ed. D. N. Freedman and J. C. Greenfield (Garden City, N.Y.: Doubleday & Co., 1969) 101-16; idem, "The Qumran Psalms Scroll (11QPs^a) Reviewed," in *On Language, Culture and Religion*, ed. M. Black and W. Smalley (The Hague: Mouton, 1974), 79-99.

18. Y. Yadin, *Megillat ha-Miqdash*, 3 vols. with supplement (Jerusalem: Israel Exploration Society, 1977).

19. Ibid., 1: 298-300.

20. Suggested orally by my former student, Merrill Miller of Wesleyan University.

13

copies the style of Deuteronomy and employs its sources much the same dynamic way the Deuteronomists employed their ancient extrabiblical sources in penning Deuteronomy.

If this is the case, the canon at Qumran was open-ended in ways considerably more radical, so far as we now know, than for any other Jewish denomination of the period. Others kept the Hagiographa open, as Sundberg has shown Christianity indeed did; but, if Yadin is correct, the Essenes kept open even the question of the canon of the Torah!

This brings forth the observation that all communities of the Book have held the concept of canon more lightly than conciliar modes of thinking admit. Undebatable is the observation that all have had various levels of canonical authority.[21] The Torah was the most canonical, so to speak, and the earliest stabilized into a clear form and shape. Next were the prophetic books, and finally the Writings, or Hagiographa. But no one ever stopped there. Just as the Essenes apparently added to the Torah and Hagiographa, so the early Christians by 100 viewed the traditions about Christ, plus some Pauline correspondence, as being authoritative to the point of being canonical.[22] They surely did not view the gospels as on the level of the Hagiographa (*Ketubim*), to be seen as having the same sort of authority as Job or the Psalms, but rather as being as important as the Torah itself.[23] Paul even claimed the Torah in certain respects (its law codes) had been abrogated and superseded by the work of God in Christ.[24]

Nor did the communities stop there. After the matter of the Hagiographa (*Ketubim*) was more or less settled for rabbinic Judaism by 100 C.E., the Oral Torah became codified or canonized by 200 C.E. The Mishnah and Talmud have *functioned* for Judaism in precisely the same ways the Bible has functioned in the believing communities, but at an authoritative level somewhat below that of the Bible. So in Christianity creeds were developed which functioned as authoritative. Hymns outside the Psalter have functioned in a similar manner, perhaps at what one might call a tertiary level of canonicity. Certainly the *Hodayot* (1Q and 4QH) would have so functioned at Qumran, but similar liturgical collections grow up in all denominations which reach a certain level not only of authority but of canonicity in the sense that they become difficult

21. Sid A. Leiman, *The Canonization of Hebrew Scripture* (Hamden: Archon, 1976). See my review in *JBL* 96 (1977): 590–91.

22. James A. Sanders, "Text and Canon: Old Testament and New," in *Mélanges Dominique Barthélemy*, ed. P. Casetti, O. Keel, A. Schenker (Fribourg: Presses Universitaires, 1981), 373–94.

23. W. D. Davies, *Christian Origins and Judaism* (London: Darton, Longman and Todd, 1962); James A. Sanders, "Torah and Christ," *Int.* 29 (1975): 372–90.

24. James A. Sanders, "Torah and Paul," in *God's Christ and His People: Studies in Honor of Nils Alstrup Dahl* (Oslo: Universitetsforlaget, 1977), 132–40.

to change because they attain a certain status in the communities which revere and use them. All this bespeaks the essentially conservative nature of communities of faith and belief. Even certain translations, such as the Septuagint (LXX) of the OT for early Christians, the Vulgate of Jerome for very conservative Roman Catholics, or the King James Version still for many Christians, attain a certain canonical status.

Biblical canons depend for content and order on the denomination or communion in view. The ecumenical movement has raised our consciousness to see that there is a plurality of canons in the several Christian communions. It is very difficult now to think about canon, either as it was in antiquity or as it is today, in parochial or singularist modes. Pluralism is a part of responsible perception of the concept of canon.[25]

The Scrolls have caused a review of the formation and history of the OT text, as well as of canon.[26] Basic now is a four-stage history: the period of the *Urtext*, the period of the Accepted Texts, the period of the Received Text, and finally, the Massoretic Text (MT). Reconstruction of the *Urtext* is not within the competence or province of text criticism: that entails the tools of higher criticism, as the expression goes, and not those of lower or textual criticism. So far as we know there is no autograph extant of any biblical writing, and text criticism deals with extant texts and versions.

But the salient observation of the newly revised history of the text comes in the second period, that of the Accepted Texts from around 300 B.C.E. to about 100 C.E. Pluralism is the key again to accurate perception of the available data. At that point where we have actual biblical texts in hand, beginning in the Hellenistic period, the oldest apparently dating to the third century B.C.E., we have a pluralistic picture. We had known from the LXX that the Greek-speaking Jewish communities actually had quite different texts in translation of certain books than the Hebrew-speaking communities. There are remarkable differences between the LXX and MT of 1 and 2 Samuel, Jeremiah, Esther, Daniel, Proverbs, and Ezekiel 40—48. And there are on a lesser level numerous very important differences in books such as Isaiah and Job. Before the discovery of the

---

25. James A. Sanders, "The Bible as Canon," *CC* 98:39 (1981): 1250-55.

26. Moshe Greenberg, "The Stabilization of the Text of the Hebrew Bible, Reviewed in the Light of the Biblical Materials from the Judean Desert," *JAOS* 76 (1956): 157-67. Shermaryahu Talmon, "Aspects of the Textual Transmission of the Bible in the Light of Qumran Manuscripts," *Textus* 4 (1964): 95-132. Moshe H. Goshen-Gottstein, "Hebrew Biblical Manuscripts, Their History and Their Place in the HUBP Edition," *Biblica* 48 (1967): 243-90. Dominique Barthélemy, s.v. "Text, Hebrew, History of," IDB Sup; idem, "Histoire du texte hébraïque de l'Ancien Testament, in *Etudes d'histoire du texte de l'Ancien Testament* (Fribourg: Presses Universitaires, 1978), 341-64. See also the several articles by Talmon, Goshen-Gottstein, Cross, Barthélemy, myself, and others collected in *Qumran and the History of the Biblical Text* (Cambridge, Mass.: Harvard Univ. Press, 1975). All this is reviewed and a synthesis advanced in James A. Sanders, "Text and Canon: Concepts and Method," *JBL* 98 (1979): 5-29.

Scrolls it was difficult to know whether most of these should be seen primarily as translational, or as reflecting the inner history of the Septuagint text, or as reflecting an interesting early history of the Hebrew text, or all three. Now it is abundantly clear that the second period of text transmission, actually that of the earliest texts we have, was one of limited textual pluralism. Side by side in the Qumran library lay scrolls of Jeremiah in Hebrew dating to the pre-Christian Hellenistic period reflecting both the textual tradition known in the MT and the one in the LXX, without any indication of preference.[27] So also for 1 and 2 Samuel.[28]

These observations have led to two distinct theories about the pluralism of the period. The one would see in the period three families of texts—the Babylonian which became the MT, the Egyptian which was the base of the LXX, and the Palestinian which would have included the Samaritan Pentateuch and the Hebrew base of certain Greek translational traditions.[29] The other theory holds that there was in the second period a main stream of Hebrew textual tradition with rivulets running parallel to it.[30] Each has first-rate textual scholars arguing the case. But common to both theories is the observation of pluralism in the second period with a process of standardization and stabilization beginning in the first century B.C.E. and moving with acceleration through the first century C.E. until complete by the end of the first century.[31] While the older texts from Qumran demonstrate the fluidity and pluralism of the second period, the later texts from caves discovered elsewhere in the Judaean desert, dating from the end of the first century up to the second Jewish revolt, show the result of the stabilization process: the latter are in effect proto-Massoretic texts of the period of the Received Text with remarkably few variants over against the great MT manuscripts of the ninth and tenth centuries C.E. We had no way of knowing these crucial facts before the discovery a third of a century ago of the Dead Sea Scrolls. The dramatic change comes between the second and third periods, that is, with the manuscripts dating after 70 C.E.; or, to put it

27. J. Gerald Janzen, *Studies in the Text of Jeremiah* (Cambridge, Mass.: Harvard Univ. Press, 1973); Emanuel Tov, *The Septuagint Translation of Jeremiah and Baruch* (Missoula, Mont.: Scholars Press, 1976). See also Richard D. Weis's 1980 SBL paper, "Jeremiah 34(41): 8–22. A Probe into the Formation of the Book of Jeremiah," (unpublished; see chap. 3 n. 2).

28. E.C. Ulrich, *The Qumran Text of Samuel and Josephus* (Missoula, Mont.: Scholars Press, 1978); Emanuel Tov, *The Text-Critical Use of the Septuagint in Biblical Research* (Jerusalem: Simor, 1981).

29. Frank M. Cross, "The History of the Biblical Text in the Light of Discoveries in the Judaean Desert," *HTR* 57 (1964): 281–99.

30. See above, n. 26, the Talmon and Goshen-Gottstein articles. See also the introduction to *The Book of Isaiah: Sample Edition with Introduction* by M. H. Goshen-Gottstein (Jerusalem: Magnes, 1965), 11–20, esp. 17.

31. Dominique Barthélemy, *Les Devanciers d'Aquila* (Leiden: E. J. Brill, 1963); Sanders, "Text and Canon: Concepts and Method," (see n. 26 above).

another way, the change is notable between the biblical manuscripts from Qumran, all of which date before 70, and those from the other sites where scrolls have been discovered in the area since the 1950s, including those found at Masada in the early 1960s.

Limited pluralism and fluidity are the salient marks of both text *and* canon, therefore, in the Hellenistic pre-70 period, precisely the era we call early Judaism which was marked also by a pluralism of Jewish denominations and various expressions of religious experience. We can no longer speak of a standard, orthodox, or normative Judaism with contemporary, aberrant, or heterodox Jewish sects in early Judaism. Nor can we think of a standard, normative text of the Bible deriving directly from an authentic (conjectured) *Urtext* with contemporary, aberrant, or heterodox texts sponsored by the aberrant sects that perhaps used them. Nor can we think of a mostly stable canon of the *Ketubim*, as of Esther or Proverbs or Psalms, or certainly of the corpus as a whole, with aberrant sectarian collections on the side—with a Council of Jamnia settling it all and putting the aberrant sects in their place once for all.

The whole picture of early Judaism is different from what had been supposed until the discovery of the Scrolls. The notion of there having been a normative Judaism of the period valiantly carrying the torch of continuity between the early postexilic period and the earliest rabbinic literature datable to the early common era, with deviations arising from time to time but finally dying out under the blows of the two Jewish revolts of 66–69 and 132–135 C.E., thus proving their essential errancy, was a picture born of the principle of "economy of explanation." No scholar has painted the picture in so bold a way, but the supposition of such a picture lies behind a great deal of the literature dealing with the period—until recently. Sometimes economy of explanation may operate to provide working hypotheses to try to account for available data, but the opposite principle is considerably more likely to produce hypotheses faithfully reflective of real human situations in antiquity, as of today. The principle of injecting the "ambiguity of reality" into working hypotheses and making it an essential part of them is considerably more likely to render such hypotheses productive and capable of accounting for available data—especially where considerable data exist as is the case now for early Judaism.

Canonical criticism is developing into a discipline of tools for handling the data pertinent to painting a reliable portrait of the reality of the canonical process in early Judaism, which issued in the received Bibles of Judaism and Christianity. It draws great strength from cognate

17

disciplines also attuned to the literature of the period, especially tradition criticism and comparative midrash.

Study of the Bible as canon is clearly an issue of biblical criticism. Brevard Childs feels strongly that his work of reviewing the Bible in full canonical context should not be thought of as a part of historical criticism. He says, "The approach which I am advocating has been described by others as 'canonical criticism'. I am not happy with this term because it implies that the concern with canon is viewed as another historical-critical technique which can take its place alongside of source criticism, form criticism, rhetorical criticism, and the like. I do not envision the approach to canon in this light. Rather, the issue at stake turns on establishing a stance from which the Bible is to be read as Sacred Scripture."[32] He appends a footnote rightly attributing the phrase canonical criticism to the writer.[33] And I fully agree that our common concern with canon cannot be reduced to another technique. It is indeed a stance from which to read the Bible. And that is the reason I say canonical criticism rather than canon criticism, because it, more than any mode yet developed for proper exegesis, includes a clear posture with regard to the Bible. Biblical criticism is itself a stance, which, however, needs an inner corrective. In short, canonical criticism, which is still growing and developing, provides both a set of tools for reading the Bible through understanding the canonical process in antiquity and a means of revitalizing and reviving the very concept of canon as the book of the churches and synagogues.

We are aware that most biblical critics in these past 250 years have retained their religious identity, whether Jewish or Christian. They have remained in the household of faith as persons. But many have done so with considerable personal tension. Canonical criticism might be that next step which permits them to reintegrate the Bible in their thinking into its own intrinsic wholeness. Form criticism takes as a basic tenet that the Bible in all its several literary units was shaped in the liturgical and instructional life of early believing communities, whether the early small literary units or the largest ones. It was born and shaped "in church" so to speak. Canonical criticism takes that seriously not just as a technique but as a stance, according to Childs. In *Introduction to the Old Testament as Scripture* Childs contends that a basic characteristic of the canonical approach in regard to both its literary and textual levels is its concern to describe the literature in terms of its relation to the historic Jewish

32. Brevard Childs, "The Canonical Shape of Prophetic Literature," *Int.* 32 (1978): 54.
33. James A. Sanders, *Torah and Canon* (Philadelphia: Fortress Press, 1972), ix; see the French ed., *Identité de la Bible* (Paris: Cerf, 1975), 9.

community rather than seeing its goal to be the reconstruction of the most original literary form of the books, or the most pristine form of a textual tradition.[34] That is very well said.

Canonical criticism might be viewed as a confession on the part of biblical criticism that it now recognizes that the true *Sitz im Leben* today of the Bible is in the believing communities—heirs to the first shapers of this literature—whatever the provenance (e.g., liturgical or instructional) of the original forms and early literary units. This development may bring the guild of biblical critics to a posture of scientific honesty and humility with regard to its own work. Gerald T. Sheppard says, "Little wonder that once the biblical text has been securely anchored in the historical past by 'decanonizing' it, the interpreter has difficulty applying it to the modern religious context."[35] That, too, is very well said. The Bible's own integrity lies in its very nature as canon. To ignore that fact or to be shy of it because the critic prefers his or her primary credentials to be in the academy is not scrupulous but unscientific in the full meaning of that term. A major tenet of historical criticism has been the observation that the Bible is a product of history. And that is right. But it is a product of a very peculiar history, the essential characteristic of which must not be overlooked, and a history which continues today in Jewish and Christian believing communities.

Canonical criticism is therefore not just another critical exercise. It is not only a logical evolution of earlier stages in the growth of criticism but it also reflects back on all the disciplines of biblical criticism and informs them all to some extent. Canonical criticism is dependent on all that has gone before in this line, but what has gone before may now be dependent to some extent on canonical criticism. If biblical criticism is to be redeemed from its own failings and from the serious charges being leveled against it, it should embrace this additional disciplinary and self-critical stance.

An aspect of the very ground of biblical criticism—that which nurtured it through these 250 years as an endeavor within traditional religious identity—was the marriage of academia and ecclesia in the Enlightenment. Strictly humanistic stances were taken in the study of the origins of "the faith." Currently some secular theologians who are openly turning away from the Bible as understood by biblical criticism are also saying that academia and ecclesia have been divorced, and the children do not know with which parent they want to stay.[36] I disagree.

34. Brevard Childs, *Introduction*, 57-68.
35. Cited in Childs' *Introduction*, 79. See Gerald T. Sheppard, "Canon Criticism: The Proposal of Brevard Childs and an Assessment for Evangelical Hermeneutics," *Studia Biblica et Theologica* 4 (1974): 3-17; and his *Wisdom as a Hermeneutical Construct* (New York: Walter de Gruyter, 1980).

Historical study of the Bible might indeed be thought of as study of what the Spirit was doing in all the earlier "nows" of biblical history.

Recanonizing the Bible, so to speak, places it back where it belongs, in the believing communities of today. It re-presents the Bible. But canonical criticism, insofar as it does that, can bring with it into the churches the exciting results of criticism to date. It can make the academy more at ease in church and synagogue because it can assist the academy to cease and desist from unscientific and unenlightened attitudes toward them. Canonical criticism might be seen in metaphor as the beadle (*bedelos*) who now carries the critically studied Bible in procession back to the church lectern from the scholar's study. And canonical criticism may permit the current believing communities to see themselves more clearly as heirs of a very long line of shapers and reshapers of tradition and instruct the faithful as to how they may faithfully perceive the Bible even yet as adaptable for life. Finally, it might help reduce the gap between pulpit and pew and permit pastors to be more honest in their preaching and teaching.

36. An oral communication by a former colleague.

II

Canonical Process

Canonical criticism has two major foci. The one may be called the canonical process and the other canonical hermeneutics.

Some current scholars, recognizing both that the discipline is necessary and that its time has come, seem to prefer the expression canon criticism for the whole endeavor.[1] At first blush it is a term with which scholarship would seem more at ease, for the expression *canonical criticism*, they say, can be misunderstood to say that criticism is canonical. There may be that risk. But we say historical criticism, textual criticism, rhetorical criticism and even structural criticism, without feeling the danger of conveying the impression that we think criticism to be, say, rhetorical or historical. Also there is reluctance to use the term because some scholars feel that the matter of biblical authority falls properly outside the province of historical study. I suspect that this plays a major role with some. The sociology of knowledge, however, has now brought us to recognize that scholars themselves have systems of values of which they should be fully conscious, and that when they are so aware they are better equipped to see that to omit the question of authority, ancient or modern, from their work is to fall short of being fully scientific. The very concept of canon has a present aspect as well as a historical one. To continue to avoid that observation, as biblical criticism has wanted to do since its early adherents tried to limit its purview, is to continue to ignore the problems it has given rise to and to try to evade the challenges recently leveled against it.

The history of canon, or the canonical process, as an element in canonical criticism, includes both a particular perspective and a set of tools and techniques. It uses tools common to other subdisciplines of biblical criticism but uses them differently because of the perspective. Above all the process requires questions the other subdisciplines tend

1. Such as Gerald Sheppard (see chap. 1 n. 35) and Albert Outler, "Gospel Studies' in Transition," in *The Relationship Among the Gospels*, 24, and n. 18.

not to ask. It stresses the nature and function of canon, and the process by which canon was shaped in antiquity, not solely as shaped at the end of a history of literary formation, but as shaped from the earliest moments when repetition of a "value" rendered it a tradition down to a final, ordered collection of those traditions.

A primary character of canon is its *adaptability* as well as its *stability*. These two qualities must be seen together and in the same light. The concept of canon in terms of its *function* in the believing communities puts in relief the rather amazing fact of *repetition*. Repetition of a community value in a context other than that of its "original" provenance (the main stress of biblical criticism until recently) introduces the possibility, some would say the necessity, of *resignification* of that value to some limited extent. One may have been able to repeat the value (probably literary in oral form) "accurately," meaning in this instance verbatim, but the very fact that the later context involved different ears, questions, and concerns means the high likelihood that a somewhat different meaning was derived from rereading the text (*relecture*, the French call it). In other words the value needed by the repeating-reciting community may have been the same as in the original instance or it may have been different; but in both instances the tradition had to be able to speak to the new occasion or it would not have been repeated. Hence the character of the value was both to some extent *stable* and to some extent *adaptable*. If it had been too narrowly conceived in the first place, or too rigid, it might not have been repeated—hence would not have started its journey toward traditionhood, then canon.

This is not to say that every small literary unit in the Bible is highly multivalent. All really good literature, especially poetry, is multivalent or capable of saying different things to different people at different times. Naturally, one can isolate a passage, such as the list of David's mighty men (2 Sam. 23:8–39), of very low *multivalency*; but even there one cannot be sure that the recital of such a list might not have meant different things to the ancient communities, according to the salient needs of those communities at the times of repetition, *even if* at an early stage it was originally just a roster. There is perhaps a law operative here: the less multivalency in such an isolated passage the more stable the value for the historian. But to recite 2 Samuel 23 in its entirety, just to broaden the literary unit only a bit, and not to speak of the larger literary context of Samuel-Kings, puts that list of men in a certain light. They were men over whom David, the anointed of the God of Jacob and the sweet psalmist of Israel (RSV), ruled (23:1–3), the opposite of godless men who like thorns are thrown away (23:6). In the slightly fuller context of 2 Samuel 22—24, it then becomes very clear that David and the mighty men, for all their strength and valiant character, had their true value only in the plans and work of God. Breaking the Bible down into small isolated units for purposes of reconstructing history, for instance, can miss what has given and continues to give the Bible canonical value for the believing communities. The full canonical context can no longer be overlooked, and it will always yield a theological, even theocentric observation, with perhaps an eschatological dimension.

Canonical criticism makes such observations, but it also stresses the very pertinent and important observation that even small literary units, whether isolated according to modern form-critical rules or according to the rules of ancient exegetes when they isolated whatever passage they needed, have some measure of multivalency. Even repetition of the list of David's mighty men by itself can mean different things in different contexts, according to the salient questions in the minds of the community—recalling past glory to retain present identity, or anticipation of reestablishment of the monarchy, or expectations in an eschatological context, or challenge by a Judas Maccabaeus, perhaps, to keep the troops in tow. I have pursued the case of the mighty men only to make the major point of *multivalency*. In other passages it would be much easier to demonstrate. Proverbs are notoriously multivalent. All good poetry is to some measure ambiguous. Myth is by nature multivalent and adaptable to many situations: one needs but to look at how many different meanings scholars in the past 200 years, with all their analytical tools, have claimed was *the* original meaning of Genesis 2—3. Even scholars are subject to the *Zeitgeist* of whatever age in which they live: it is a part of the limitation as well as gift of humanity.

One of the observations derived from other critical disciplines which becomes important here is that of adaptability in the preliterary history of a tradition. Prior to stabilization in a certain literary form the context of most traditions was adaptable to different literary forms. Content could often be poured, as it were, into the literary form suitable to an occasion. An aspect of the Bible's *pluralism* is the fact that it includes numerous cases of precisely that. These are common observations: Samuel-Kings is largely repeated in a different literary context in Chronicles, with portions of it repeated in the different literary contexts of Isaiah (36—39) and Jeremiah (52). Psalm 18 functions one way in the Psalter but in a different way as 2 Samuel 22 in the context of Samuel-Kings. Another common observation of this type is in the doublets and triplets in Genesis: the same story of a patriarch and matriarch going for aid to a foreign country with the same threat to their marriage and, more important, to God's promise of great progeny for them, is told three times. The story is highly adaptable. There are four Gospels in the New Testament, a gold mine for studying the Bible's *pluralism and multivalency*.[2]

What Jesus said to the disciples was apparently adaptable to many different early church congregations. And we can only be grateful that we inherit the four instead of Tatian's Diatesseron which attempted to harmonize them and unify them for a church or perhaps even several churches at a particular time in the fourth century. Paul's letters were clearly written, each of them, to very particular situations in the middle third of the first century. But we can be sure we would simply not have inherited them in the manner we have, by tradition in the churches through the centuries instead of discovery by archaeology, had other early churches not found value in them for themselves in different times and contexts. *Ecce!* Churches in the twentieth century continue to find value in them. All this matter of *stability-adaptability*, *pluralism*, *multivalency*, *repetition-recitation*, and *resignification* are proper focuses of study for canonical criticism. Very important also is regard for the inherent *constraints* within a text. As we shall see, in the next chapter, it is simply not canonically fair to bring extraneous hermeneutics to the text to make it say what clearly violates a plain (*peshat*) reading.

Canonical criticism focuses on the *function* of authoritative traditions in the believing communities, early or late. It is not uninterested in literary structure and does not denigrate those disciplines which focus on structure, such as form criticism, redaction criticism, and structural analysis, or which focus on the final form of the text. Close attention to textual structure may indicate proper function. But, in consonance with later emphases in tradition criticism and especially comparative midrash, canonical criticism stresses what the function of a tradition, in whatever form it is found, had when called on for his or her community by a tradent. What authority or value did the tradent seek in the tradition? How did he or she use it?

Brevard Childs speaks of how canon may have functioned and may still function today in the believing communities, but he does so singularly emphasizing the final form of the text. Childs seeks the theological movement integral to a text once it is located in the larger canonical context, and he especially asks what each biblical book

2. Eugene Lemcio, "The Gospels and Canonical Criticism," *BTB* 11 (1981): 114–22; and my response, ibid., 122–24.

conveys in its fullness with all the smaller literary units of its makeup seen each in relation to the other, and how each functions relating to the others. Childs stresses the important point that the Bible as a whole is far more than the sum of its parts, but he does his work principally on each book of the Bible, putting back together what the form and tradition critics rent asunder. And that is important. But when Childs uses the word *function* in this regard he means in literary context; the consolation of Deutero-Isaiah canonically and theologically must be seen in relation to the castigations of the First Isaiah when the sixty-six chapters are seen as a whole; then, if one does so, one sees a fuller theological statement, or Word, as it might or should function for later believing communities.

Canonical criticism is very interested in what a believing community had in mind at that passing moment when the final form was achieved, but it does not focus so much on that form as does Childs. For no sooner did the text become stabilized into the forms which we inherit (some books had several forms and some communities have had different books in different orders) but that it was rendered adaptable by numerous hermeneutic techniques brought to bear on it in order to crack it open once more to derive needed value from it. It would appear that once the text became frozen into a final form—there were numerous "final" forms—the communities soon found the hermeneutic means necessary to break it down to reapply to their purposes and needs.[3] Of course, they may all share a certain broadly conceived "biblical theology"—God as Creator, Judge, Redeemer, and Sustainer—but that can be seen in numerous early small literary units as well, and may be more clearly seen in a Greek Esther than a Hebrew Esther.

Biblical criticism has established itself and its legitimacy largely on its developing ability to explain Scripture. In Enlightenment terms this has meant the recovery of the original intent of the author or the understanding of the original audience. By contrast, canon functions to explain for the community that finds its identity in it an otherwise obscure and disorderly, even inexplicable, world; it is not the "world," even the world of the scholar, that explains canon.[4] There was a radical shift here directly attributable to biblical criticism. It was a shift in stance or attitude that is very important to circumscribe in order to understand the nature of midrash as well as the concept of canon. It is Scripture as canon which explains the world in the ambiguity of reality.

3. James A. Sanders, "Canonical Context and Canonical Criticism," *HBT* 2 (1980): 173-97.
4. See my review of Raymond E. Brown's *The Birth of the Messiah* (Garden City, N.Y.: Doubleday & Co., 1977) in *USQR* 33 (1978): 193-96.

A new approach to the study of early Jewish interpretation of Scripture, *comparative midrash*[5] began to emerge in the 1950s. *Midrash* is a Hebrew word, found already in the Hebrew Bible, which basically means "quest." It comes from the verb *darash* which means "seek." In early biblical idiom one sought God or a word from the deity, an oracle or answer to a question: one sought divine will for decision making. This was done by kings as well as common folk, prophets, and priests. The means of addressing the quest varied considerably. If one sought the presence of the deity it was usually in a theophanic context, but it could be less dramatic. Prophets tended to emphasize a living dynamic expression of the divine will for the inquirer while priests sometimes had some technique and perhaps instrument by which to seek an answer, such as the ephod, urim, and thummim.

As time went on traditions accumulated from earlier such decisions which were called *torot*, teachings or instruction, both for prophet and priest. It is at this point that canonical criticism through the developing study of intrabiblical midrash becomes interested in what went on— precisely the employment of the same tradition in a second situation. Comparative midrash attempts to ferret out all passages in the Bible, and, of course, the later literature, in which an earlier tradition is called upon. Comparative midrash, as a tool of canonical criticism, listens carefully to the tradition critics at this point, insofar as the tradition critic shows interest in *how* that tradition was called on and for what purpose.

One of the keys to proper understanding at this point is to remember to think of midrash as "quest" rather than as it is usually translated, "interpretation" or "explanation." This is important in order to have the right understanding of this crucial stage of the *canonical process* which had begun in earliest biblical times. Midrash was the mode whereby in biblical and later antiquity one explained the world by received tradition properly brought to bear on the situation for which wisdom was sought. It was the world or one's condition which needed illumination, clarification, and explanation; and that was what canonical tradition was for, to make sense of what was going on. Of course, this did not mean that the tradition was always patent and obvious, far from it. One always had to determine the sense of a tradition, and there were always hermeneutic axioms and rules whereby to do so. But the sense or meaning was sought not as a thing in itself, as biblical criticism insists on doing out of its respect for the text, but rather as illumination on life. It is

5. Perhaps the most succinct statement of meaning and method is Roger Le Déaut's "A Propos a Definition of Midrash," *Int.* 25 (1971): 259–82; Trans. Mary Howard Calloway, from *Biblica* 50 (1969): 395–413.

a matter of attitude, and we children of the Enlightenment need to have our consciousness raised a bit in this regard. Tradition and hence canon was not an *object* per se of study for clarification by other extracanonical means, such as tools of exegesis. It was the means whereby one sought truth and wisdom for a particular problem or situation. In this sense the *object* was the world, not Scripture and tradition. Our use of critical, exegetic tools in reading a text is in part for the purpose of seeing how this happened.

Study of the history of such quests first within the Bible and then in postbiblical literature is revealing indeed. One first learns in such study that midrash, understood in this broad sense, extends back into biblical times—almost as far as one can go. From earliest times, it would appear, the believing community contemporized earlier value-traditions to their own situation. A priori one must also say that traditions had origins at a point before they became such. On the other hand, the study of the function of traditions, even in early biblical times, by no means denies the spontaneous sort of revelation that the Bible claims for some of its great figures. Both of these restrictions must be kept in mind. The Bible—as we have it—is a veritable textbook in contemporization of tradition. Some of the oldest material in the Bible, as received, contemporized tradition for a new (ancient) situation. From our point of view, the prophets, who are frequently thought of as original thinkers and even as spontaneous oracles in their own right, are now seen to be citing, either directly or by allusion, authoritative traditions of the communities to which they spoke.[6] We have called those traditions part of the Torah story;[7] others call them Israel's epic traditions or recitals. Since the 1930s form criticism and tradition criticism have ferreted them out of the various strata of the Bible for all to see.[8] In short, even the great prophets who claimed to be able to quote God directly in fresh revelation also quoted earlier core traditions of the community to validate their message. This does not mean that they were only reactionary or conservative, as some have claimed because of the results of form-critical work, but they certainly honored and used tradition considerably more than earlier studies have indicated.[9]

6. See, for instance, Walter Brueggemann, *The Prophetic Imagination* (Philadelphia: Fortress Press, 1978).

7. In *Torah and Canon*; see also "Torah and Christ," 372-90.

8. Beginning with Gerhard von Rad's seminal 1938 essay: "The Form-Critical Problem of the Hexateuch," in *The Problem of the Hexateuch and Other Essays* (New York: McGraw-Hill, 1966), 1-78.

9. See George E. Mendenhall, "Biblical History in Transition," in *The Bible and the Ancient Near East*, ed. G. Ernest Wright (Garden City, N.Y.: Doubleday & Co., 1961), 27-58. See my critique in "Adaptable for Life: The Nature and Function of Canon," in *Magnalia Dei: The Mighty Acts of God*, ed. F. M. Cross et al. (Garden City, N.Y.: Doubleday, 1976), 531-60.

The prophets used tradition "canonically." But so did other ancient biblical tradents whose works ended up in the Bible. These observations are important in studying canon, for we can now see that there has been a continuum of function of canonical literature in the believing communities from earliest times to latest. What changed along that line were factors such as the gradual stabilization of tradition into scripture, from Torah materials down through the Writings and beyond, the establishment of the full concept of Torah in early Judaism, the intense stabilization process which went on for Judaism in the first centuries B.C.E. and C.E., the change in ontology of canon that took place in the same time frame, and the development of the hermeneutics necessary to render what had become stable, pliable, and flexible and adaptable to ever-changing contexts and problems.

But all along that line was a *quest*, by the believing communities, put to the traditions—whether oral, written, fluid, or stable—in constantly changing circumstances. And that quest was for the most part of two major sorts. As history changed and the fortunes of the people, even their habitats and customs changed, they needed to know ever anew *who they were and what they should do.* The function of tradition-scripture-canon has always largely been to answer for the believing communities the two essential and existential questions of *identity* and *lifestyle.* That is the reason Torah, even in its strictest and shortest and most authoritative form, the Pentateuch, includes laws, even though it is obviously and basically a story of the origins of the world and of Israel. It not only reminded Israel and Judah and the early churches who they were and in whose land and world they lived but also did not leave them without some fairly clear precepts of how they should conduct themselves in that world and in that land.

Actually the whole of the canon can be loosely but faithfully characterized as a story full of adaptable wisdom on how to live at any time. The story is amazingly theocentric in the way it is told, no matter the several sources, early and late, which went into its composition. In canonical perspective it is basically God's story.[10] It is full of the verbs of God's words and actions. God does the creating, the electing, the guiding, the judging, the redeeming, the sustaining, and the re-creating—according to the story. No exclusively historical or humanistic reading of the canon can fully appreciate its story or what it has to say.

This observation brings us back to a weakness we observed in the ways biblical criticism has tended to read the Bible. Insofar as criticism

---

10. James A. Sanders, *God Has a Story Too* (Philadelphia: Fortress Press, 1979).

reads the Bible solely as a product of history, it shares the limitations of humanism: it can only ask what the contributors to the Bible back then believed their God was saying and doing. That is precisely what it ought to ask, and is perhaps all it ought to ask of the Bible in the scholar's study. But if academia and ecclesia are truly wed, then the same scholar who is also a member of a believing community should go on, for the sake of the community, to ask what the story—when all the various bits and pieces of whatever provenance are juxtaposed in and as canon—says is the way God speaks and acts. There is then a dimension to the whole which is far more than the several parts or the sum of those parts.

That dimension is a canonical dimension which cannot be attributed to any discreet genius, such as author or editor or redactor, in the past. It can only be attributed to the ancient communities which continued to find value in the received traditions and scriptures, generation after generation, passing them on for the value they had found in them. Redaction criticism cannot be the final stage of growth of biblical criticism. As Brevard Childs wisely says, "A hiatus remains between the shape given the material by the last literary source and its final canonical shape."[11] Rolf Rendtorff rightly senses a problem with critical solutions so far offered to the formation of the Pentateuch.[12] He has recently tried to show that the received form of the Pentateuch cannot be attributed either to traditional connections in the oral stage or to the literary sources, J or P. Childs picks up on that observation and says:

In my judgment, Rendtorff's analysis allows one to draw some important canonical observations. The final form of the Pentateuch, which cannot be simply derived from the combinations of literary sources, gives evidence of a canonical reading of the whole in its final stage or editing. The various parts were more closely united by means of cross references, either to the promises of the past or to an anticipation of the future. In sum, a theological force which reflects a knowledge of the whole Pentateuch has given it a final order.[13]

Unfortunately Childs does not say more about the theological force, but one thinks of S. Talmon's idea of continuing scribal activity after the work of the so-called final redactors in other parts of the Bible as well.[14] And, on another level, one thinks of the work of the Holy Spirit in that process. Everyone has probably had the experience of discovering new meaning even in something he or she had earlier written. We are all

11. Childs, *Introduction*, 132.
12. Rolf Rendtorff, *Das Überlieferungsgeschichtliche Problem des Pentateuch* (New York and Berlin: Walter de Gruyter, 1977).
13. See n. 11 above.
14. Shemaryahu Talmon, "The Textual Study of the Bible—A New Outlook," *Qumran and the History of the Biblical Text*, 321–400.

conduits of the insights of others in our communities. Individuals may be effective vehicles or conduits of the experiences of a whole community—synthesizers of vision who are not aware of all the meaning and value in their utterances until much later, or perhaps not at all.

It is very important at this point not to posit some further single genius as final canonical redactor, as Childs seems to do. The hiatus canonical criticism focuses on is that between the work of the last discreet geniuses, whose hands are discernible in the Bible by the tools of literary criticism, and the stable texts and canons which emerge in the third period of text transmission after 100 C.E. That hiatus cannot be filled by conjectured discreet geniuses despite our modern need to think of individual responsibility as more valid than community responsibility. It was in such periods that the faithful of believing communities, leaders and followers, shaped what they received in ways that rendered it most meaningful and valuable for them. Such periods we have chosen to call periods of intense canonical process.

The periods of *intense canonical process* were the sixth century B.C.E. and the first C.E., with the periods of early Judaism and early Christianity contributing to the process. The signal point here is that canonical criticism shifts the focus of attention on canonization away from councils to a historical process. Childs puts it very well, "The issue at stake is the nature of the process by which Israel shaped and was shaped by those traditions whose divine authority was experienced, accepted and confessed."[15] He is even clearer in a critique of the work of Walther Zimmerli with whose work on Ezekiel he largely agrees. Zimmerli, in contrast to other modern commentators of Ezekiel, takes seriously the so-called secondary passages in the Ezekiel book as presenting the opportunity to see the *Nachleben* or continuing life of a word from the prophet. Such amplification in the Ezekiel text resulted from a process in which later hands worked on the original text in the light of other passages of Scripture and of new historical events.

But Childs nonetheless criticizes Zimmerli sharply as having "missed the significance of the canonical process in which the experience of Israel with the use of its authoritative writings has been incorporated into the text itself as part of the biblical witness. . . . Zimmerli disregards this fundamental canonical decision by substituting a precanonical stage in the text's development for the normative canonical text, and by judging a significant part of the canonical text as merely commentary." A more serious charge is his second one. "Secondly,

15. Childs, *Introduction*, 172.

Zimmerli's method of working from a reconstructed *Grundtext* to which has been appended commentary runs the danger of losing the inner dynamic of the full canonical passage. To divide a passage historically into stages often destroys the synchronic dimension of the text. A literary entity has an integrity of its own which is not to be identified with the sum of its parts."[16]

Childs has been consistent in his criticism of those who, like Zimmerli, in effect locate by critical tools a kind of canon within the canon to which what remains in the Bible is commentary. "The canonical shaping not only registers that history (Israel's later experience with an early tradition) by its shaping of the tradition, but it also brings that process to an end when it fixed its canon. Everything thereafter is commentary, not text."[17] Childs had made the same criticism earlier of von Rad's creeds and Ernest Wright's recitals: they created a kind of canon within the canon by means of historical criticism.[18]

All this is quite crucial to understanding the similarities and differences in our approaches. Canonical criticism in our view corrects some attitudes and suppositions of earlier subdisciplines of biblical criticism. In fact we dare to suggest that it may redeem biblical criticism from some of the charges leveled against it. But canonical criticism can be corrective (as form criticism was of purely literary criticism in the documentary hypothesis) of earlier biblical criticism only if seen as an issue of it and a natural evolution from it. Canonical criticism, therefore, differs from what Childs calls the canonical-text perspective simply because it cannot say with him that everything in some final form (whichever) of the text is text and "everything thereafter is commentary, not text." In fact, commentary and interpretation of "text" within the Bible are integral parts of the text from earlier times. Their presence in the text need not be denied by arguments from canonization or so-called end of process.

Process as understood in canonical criticism was there from the start and continues unabated through and after the periods of intense canonical process of stabilization. Old biblical theology used to debate from time to time which came first, the Exodus or the interpretation. The whole of the Bible as canon, from earliest bits to final texts (of whichever length, order, or community), is both text and interpretation, or text and commentary. As Zimmerli shows, Ezekiel himself drew on earlier traditions of ancient Israel and Judah to comment on the events of

16. Ibid., 370.
17. Ibid.
18. Childs, *Biblical Theology in Crisis* (Philadelphia: Westminster Press, 1970).

his day. His disciples continued the process more or less well. Jesus, using prophetic-eschatological hermeneutics and drawing on many OT scriptures and traditions, commented on the religious and political situations of his day. His disciples, the apostles, and the early church faithful who contributed to the NT continued the process more or less well. Well when they used the same hermeneutic axioms in similar historical contexts as he, less well when they did not.[19]

The canon is full of both tradition and interpretation from beginning to end. It has all come from and through the liturgical and instructional life of the ancient communities, especially in the periods of intense canonical process. And all that must be recognized for what historical criticism has shown it to be, both tradition and application integrally mixed. Quite normally early commentary or interpretation becomes subject later to further interpretation; some NT interpretation of OT passages are based on a previous targum of those passages. We must not be blind to the intrabiblical process of re-presentation or contemporization just because it is part of a "final canonical text."

Equally important is recognition of the open-endedness of the canon. The interpretive process begun early on properly continues unabated and with hardly a pause even after stabilization. The next generation, after stabilization was complete, sustained the same process of repetition and application that had occurred throughout biblical times. Like previous contributors to the Bible this generation took passages or canonical traditions and applied them to their situations by the hermeneutics they needed in order to derive the value needed from them. There was no dramatic shift because of canonization and people did not start reading the whole of Isaiah, all sixty-six chapters in a sweep, or all of the Psalter (the whole books on which Childs focuses) in order to apply a theological move or Word derived from a whole book to the next problem they faced. They carried on the practice of their biblical predecessors.

This is not to say that there were no shifts in modes of reading or applying tradition and Scripture, that is, in hermeneutics. For other reasons, hermeneutics did evolve and change in interesting ways, as did the very ontology of canon, but not because of or solely at the point of "canonization" or stabilization of the text into some "final" form. Canonical criticism, taking important cues from textual criticism, sees the changes the other way round: stabilization of text, content, and order

19. I posit this historical reconstruction with the same reserve we have in speaking of the person Amos and his school, or the person Jeremiah and his schools (issuing in the quite different MT and LXX records, not totally unlike the multiple gospel situation).

32

could take place because of a basic shift in ontology of canon and the growth of quite new kinds of hermeneutics because of it. This happened because of keen needs experienced in the believing communities due to real, pressing problems in society.[20]

The canonical process was basically one of *selectivity and repetition* with interpretation. Often it has been tacitly assumed that the literature we have is what early Judaism had, either in a canon or outside it. If attention was paid to the some 35 ancient literary works referred to in the Bible,[21] it was still assumed that whatever of value was in those lost books had been absorbed into literature in the Bible. Such an assumption was influential in how one looked at canonization. Canonical criticism assumes, on the contrary, that we have but a fraction of what there was available as religious literature in ancient Israel or in early Judaism. Discovery of the Judaean scrolls has caused this change in perspective. There was much literature apparently highly valued for a while which simply did not make it into a canon, significantly, into the Jewish canon. Selectivity of what was to be in the canon took place out among the people in the believing communities, not in an authoritative council. And that selectivity took place over a period of time. It was a process. Either a work was picked up and read with interest for the value to be derived from it, generation after generation, or it was left behind.

That process of *repetition* in new, later contexts, with the process of *selectivity* that went along with it, is a crucial focus of canonical criticism. No party, denomination, or hierarchy in Jerusalem or elsewhere would have had the power to foist off on the people a literature which held little meaning or value for them. This is the basic significance of the so-called criterion of *popularity* mentioned by Josephus:[22] either a tradition or literature held value for the believing communities out there where the people were or it simply was not picked up again. One generation might recommend it by instruction to the next, parents to children, but if in a real crisis or time of need it did not deliver the value needed for survival or quality of life, the children would simply not pick it up again. This process of selectivity in the believing communities is part of what is meant by the Bible's having been shaped in the liturgical and instructional life of those communities—synagogues and churches. Not only does it mean that the literary form in which we have a tradition

20. James A. Sanders, "Text and Canon: Concepts and Method," and "Text and Canon: Old Testament and New."

21. Sid Z. Leiman, *Canonization*, 16-26.

22. In *Against Apion* I, 28-46.

in the Bible is broadly liturgical or pedagogic in form because that is the way one generation had of passing tradition on to the next. It also means that only a fraction of those traditions, even traditions in Scripture or written form, survived the history of filtration by quest of and need in the communities.

What is in the canon "made it" with the believing communities that early found value in these writings and commended them to other communities and to the next generation. Eventually, once that process was secure, the communities would have begun to attribute to the several books widely used over a period of time a dimension of sanctity—authoritative tradition. Such traditions, whether early in oral form or later in written, had functioned for the communities well enough to gain a reputation of value-bearing treasure (Matt. 13:52-53). They had done it before, so to speak, for parent generations; they could do it again.

Then, once the sanctity of such reputation was transmitted along with community commendation, canon existed for the community and persisted whether or not value derived was consistent, high, low, or latent for this or that community or generation. At that point when sacredness had been superimposed by the communities, then the survival power of the sacred literature as canon was assured without its having always to prove itself.[23] Some portions of the canonical literature of the community might not then speak to the people at all in this or that context or generation: it was passed on now because of the aura achieved in its prior history and would some day again give the value quested of it. The hermeneutics required to make the sacred book or unit of literature yield the value sought might be old, new, or even strange, but it was always essential.

The ancient Jewish and Christian books not in one of the canons may then be viewed as the literature that did not "make it." This includes not only those ancient works referred to in the Bible itself as well as many others of the time simply not referred to but also, for Protestantism, the books and literary units sometimes called apocryphal, pseudepigraphal, and sectarian—our knowledge of which grows, it seems, with each new manuscript discovery. The ancient Jewish literature, of which we have copies in the original language(s) or versions but which is not in the Jewish canon of the Hebrew Bible (the Protestant OT—the shortest canon of them all, Jewish or Christian, aside from the Samaritan canon),

23. This is the point in the canonical process that Jonathan Z. Smith's work becomes interesting; see his "Sacred Persistence: Towards a Redescription of Canon," in *Approaches to Ancient Judaism: Theory and Practice*, ed. Wm. S. Green (Missoula, Mont.: Scholars Press, 1978), 11-28.

34

comes to us through either modern archaeology, or some Christian community which handed down ancient Jewish literature as canon that Pharisaic-rabbinic Judaism did not pass on.[24] The core observation of Albert Sundberg's dissertation fits at this point: the different Christian communities, which separated from parent Judaism after 70 C.E. and did not benefit from the discussions in the Jewish communities about canon, especially discussions (not conciliar decisions) at Jamnia, passed on as canonical at some level ancient Jewish books which Judaism dropped by 100 C.E.[25] This literature *we* Western Christians call deutero-canonical, apocryphal, or pseudepigraphal; but before 70 C.E. the various books among them would have been canonical at some level for one or the other pre-70 Jewish denomination or group. These continue to be regarded as canonical at some level by Roman Catholics and by the various Orthodox communions.[26] The Protestant reformers, agreeing apparently with Jerome against Augustine, attempted to narrow the OT canon to that of contemporary rabbinic Judaism; but that was a late development and entailed many forces and problems in understanding the whole matter of canon.

It is because of the several foregoing observations that canonical criticism has a serious problem with Brevard Childs' synchronic view of the Jewish canon of the Hebrew Bible. And this is not even to speak of how to make his synchronic perspective of it pertinent for Christians as canon. His synchronic view isolates the moment of stabilization of the several texts in a certain literary form as canonical. True enough, that is the form in which the Massoretes transmitted the text of the Hebrew Bible to current Jewish communities and hence to Christians in the Hebrew form of the OT (though not in terms of the order of books in the Prophets and *Ketubim* [Hagiographa] an order which varies with each manuscript family or tradition). That stabilized form of the text became frozen as such in a particular historical context, and neither that context nor the canonical form it produced was considered binding for interpretation in later communities that read the text.

Reading the Bible in terms of full canonical context, if it means, with Childs, reading whole books, can at best be attributed perhaps to final redactors of those literary units which ended up as biblical books, or the Torah—the one section of the Bible liturgically read indeed as a whole. And it apparently had meaning for readers in the believing communities

---

24. Robert Kraft, "Christian Transmission of Greek Jewish Scriptures," in *Paganisme, Judaïsme, Christianisme* (Paris: Boccard, 1978), 207-26.
25. See chap. 1, n. 14.
26. See chap. 1, n. 16.

in the period of canonical process when the present shapes of the books and sections became more or less stabilized. But there is actually little evidence that their ideas, as discerned by Childs, dominated later readings.

It is equally clear that before the shift to understanding the Bible as "sacred text" it had been basically understood as sacred story. Canonical criticism sponsors a revival of the idea of canon as paradigm, both of God's Word and deeds, or of nouns and verbs. It also revives the struggle of Israel and the early churches to respond by monotheizing over against the several forms of polytheism in the five culture eras through and out of which the Bible was formed and shaped. That paradigm has variously been discerned in individual verses, psalms, whole books, and even in the structure of whole divisions of the story. If Childs' literary-synchronic view of Scripture is linked at all points historically with the story it tells about God and our ancestors in the faith, thus honoring and learning from their struggles in their own contexts to pursue the Integrity of Reality, then the Bible may truly be affirmed as sacred story or paradigm.

The word *shape* came to the fore precisely among those who in the late 1960s and early 1970s began to take seriously the Bible as canon. But it has been used with different connotations. For Morton Smith it means those historical and political forces in Jewish life from the Persian to the Hellenistic period that selected the earlier literature to be canon. The Jewish political party which survived all the various challenges of those centuries was one he posits as the "Yahweh-only party," which, he claims, was in a position of sufficient political strength to make such decisions for all Jewish communities.[27] For Brevard Childs *shape* means the final theological statement or movement discernible in a biblical section, such as Torah, or a single book in its final, canonical makeup. He seems to claim that this movement is not discernible until the book or literary unit is read as a final whole—when all its so-called secondary accretions and superscriptions and the like were in place. Childs often speaks of the hermeneutical move attained in a biblical book in its full canonical context.

In canonical context, as we perceive it, the word refers to the hermeneutics which emerge from viewing the Bible canonically, not only in single books but from the Bible holistically perceived. Earlier efforts, such as the biblical theology movement, to discern the so-called

27. M. Smith, *Palestinian Parties and Politics that Shaped the Old Testament* (New York: Columbia Univ. Press, 1971).

unity of the Bible are abandoned. Canonical criticism celebrates the *pluralism* of the Bible and stresses its self-critical dimension in the varied thrusts and statements it records. There is no program that can be constructed on the basis of the Bible which can escape the challenge of other portions of it: this is an essential part of its pluralism. No one person, no denomination, no theology, and certainly no ideology can exhaust the Bible or claim its *unity*. It bears with it its own redeeming contradictions, and this is a major reason it has lasted so long and has spoken effectively to so many different historical contexts and communities. Once a theme or strain or thread rightly perceived in the Bible has been isolated and absolutized, it simply becomes available for challenge from another theme or strain also there. The whole Bible, of whichever canon, can never be stuffed into one theological box, as classically recognized by the term *biblical paradox*: the canon always contains the seed of redemption of any abuse of it.

In defiance of Marcion, who in the middle of the second century C.E. wanted to make the Bible speak with one voice, through Luke and Paul only, the communities of faith insisted on a multiple-gospel canon added to a fully diverse "Old Testament" and complemented by epistles and the Apocalypse.

Canonical criticism traces the history of the function of those authoritative traditions which ended up in one of the canons. In order to do so it uses all the valid and pertinent tools of biblical criticism, especially tradition criticism, but focuses on the believing communities at every stage along the way rather than only on the individual discreet geniuses, such as original thinkers, editors, redactors, and the like, whose hands may be evident in the process.

The tendency of biblical scholarship is to attempt to locate, even give a name to, if possible, the person in antiquity who effected the shapes of the various literary units, from smallest to largest, that emerge in the Bible. This is an apparent need of the modern scholar. It has served scholarship quite well for the most part but must now be seen as a limitation in any quest of the history of the canonical process. There may well have been one or more geniuses stationed at every point in such a history, but simply to locate them does not complete the task biblical criticism must now accomplish. One must then ask why the believing communities accepted what they did rather than set it aside, and that is crucial to determine, if the history is to be conceived and traced. We may not always succeed, for we may not have all the data we need or the tools for studying them; but we must now adjust our own thinking (our own scholarly hermeneutics, as it were) as students of the formation of the Bible, if we are to move on to the next important tasks.

The historian knows that more often than not traditions are received and accepted by a later generation for reasons quite different from the original intention.[28] Canonical criticism is interested in those later reasons, especially as they are discernible in the crucial periods of intense canonical process—that process which took place precisely between *the early acceptance and repetition* in a different context of the work of some genius, *and the later time* when such canonical works received a special aura and sanctity as imposed by the believing communities.

As I have contended, we should not assume malice aforethought in the motivations of the communities if they failed to pass on or pass down some particular literary work. In some cases there *may* have been strong reasons for setting some works aside, such as certain theological convictions which religious leaders in certain generations were able to impart to the populace at large; these need to be entertained where they arise. For the most part, however, the historical phenomenon which must impose itself on our thinking now is that the people of various communities, including *both* the leader *and* the faithful followers, either did or did not find value for themselves in this or that writing. If they did not, then we may hear no more about it until perhaps an archaeologist reports its discovery. If they did, then an intriguing history begins. Canonical criticism suggests that once the historical phenomenon occurs, the tradition or literary work has a life of its own unencumbered by the original intentions of author or redactor, or even of the first tradents, though they must all be included in the canonical history of the tradition.

Only recently have biblical scholars been able to acknowledge their claims to objectivity for what they are and to recognize the limits of such claims. All the while that objectivity was a conscious and well-meaning goal, biblical criticism was actually subscribing to a clear and distinct view of biblical authority. And that view was based on the model of the inspiration of the individual prophet.[29] Fundamentalists and liberals, that is, the opponents of biblical criticism as well as its advocates, both attributed authenticity to the original speaker or writer of whatever portion of Scripture was under purview. The only real difference

28. See, e.g., Peter R. Ackroyd, "Original Text and Canonical Text," *USQR* 32 (1977): 166-73.
29. Paul J. Achtemeier, *The Inspiration of Scripture: Problems and Proposals* (Philadelphia: Westminster Press, 1980), 99ff.

between them was that the one (the conservative) attributed more of the passage to the original individual than did the other (the liberal scholar). The conservative often would claim that every word recorded in the passage stemmed from the first writer or speaker while the biblical critic would distinguish between "genuine" and "spurious" passages, or "original" and "secondary."

Why would intelligent folk trained in history and philology want to make such distinctions in a passage of Scripture? Precisely because they desired, as historians, to reconstruct a particular moment or monument in history, namely what an author or speaker actually wrote or said. In order to do so the scholar would peel away accretions of later hands as they were discerned by use of the literary historian's tools to arrive at what the ancient contributor to the Bible had bequeathed. This is a legitimate exercise as long as its purpose and its limitations are kept clearly in mind, namely, to reconstruct a particular moment in biblical history. Unfortunately, that purpose and its limitations have not always been kept clearly in mind. On the contrary, generations of students in the mainline seminaries which sponsored and nourished biblical criticism were left with the impression that what had been peeled away was spurious and inauthentic or ungenuine for purposes other than the historian's exercise. That is, the results of historical criticism spilled over into the larger question of biblical authority.

The result was to leave the seminary student with the impression that what had been peeled away could be thrown away or set aside so far as preaching and teaching in the churches were concerned. If it was secondary historically, how could it have real authority for proclamation? Such a question carries a presupposition, namely, that only the original or most primitive words in a text held authority for the churches. The importance of this presupposition has only recently been exposed. It is one thing for the historian to work on a biblical text for the limited purpose of writing a history of the Bible and its formation, it is quite another to subscribe unconsciously or otherwise to the view that only the original words of a passage are authoritative for the churches; but that is exactly what happened to several generations of seminary students. And it was this attitude and this result of the work of the biblical critic that disturbed conservatives, especially those often called fundamentalists or literalists. They were called literalists precisely because their response to the work of biblical historical criticism was based also on the view that only the original words of the biblical author were authoritative.

In other words, those who engaged in the bitterest aspects of the fundamentalist-modernist controversy of the nineteenth and early twentieth centuries actually were in basic agreement on the question of authority: inspiration came through the individual speaker or writer in antiquity. The one may have spoken of it in terms of *revelatio specialis* and the other in terms of *revelatio generalis*, but they agreed that the authority of the biblical witness was of the individual. The difference was essentially quantitative and not qualitative, that is, how much of Scripture could be attributed to those individuals so inspired. For the literalist it was everything while for the biblical critic it was what could be called original or genuine as opposed to later additions.

Such a view, held by both sides, bypassed the believing communities in antiquity and focused on the individual in the past as indeed it did in the present. Both sides agreed that what was important today was what the individual could believe. For the evangelical it was often cast in terms of whether the individual was saved and that often depended on whether one believed "the Bible was true." For the more liberal thinker and certainly for the biblical critic there was often an existential concern for the intellectual integrity of the individual who chose to remain in the church or regain individual identity as a person of faith.

The tendency to bracket the believing community and devalue it in efforts to understand the Bible has been rather pervasive, especially in Protestant circles, whether liberal or conservative. It has been somewhat true of Catholicism as well to the extent that the latter accepts the legitimacy of biblical criticism, but for the most part the Roman Catholic Church's twofold understanding of authority, Scripture, and the Magisterium, and its traditional lectionary approach to the Bible, have until recently kept it from the tendency. Non-Roman churches that are thought of as "high church" have escaped the tendency to some extent as well, especially where the tradition of the lectionary is strong. Even so, a lectionary approach to proclamation does not prevent the preacher from viewing portions of the assigned passage as secondary if he or she was taught so in seminary.[30]

One of the results of the Reformation was to break the chains that bound the Bible to the church lectern and give the Bible to the people. In the course of the Protestant sponsorship of biblical criticism, however, the Bible never reached the people but became as firmly bound to the scholar's study as it ever had been to the church lectern. Biblical criticism made the Bible into a sort of archaeological tell which only experts could dig! A new priesthood arose to replace the old, but it seemed to be even more exclusive than the old. Consider how many languages one must

30. James A. Sanders, "Canon and Calendar: A Lectionary Proposal," in *Social Themes of the Christian Year: A Liberating Approach to the Lectionary*, ed. D. T. Hessel (Philadelphia: Geneva, 1983), 257–63.

learn, how much history one must master, and how many years it takes to earn the Ph.D. that authorizes one to be called biblical scholar.

In some seminaries nowadays, a professor of homiletics might dread preaching from the Bible in chapel in the presence of the Bible faculty. After chapel, one might hear the biblical scholar say to the preacher, "That was very nice; but apparently you did not take into account the latest scholarly reconstruction of your pericope—in light of the discoveries at Tell el-. . .!" This is an intentional caricature but nonetheless makes a point. Such a remark might deprive the sermon of its scriptural authority, but only because the two shared the presupposition noted earlier: authority would rest with the reconstructed "original" passage discerned by biblical criticism, rather than with what the early believing communities shaped and passed on.

Canonical criticism focuses on the communities that found value in what the ancient individuals produced as members of those communities, and the value they found may not have been exactly what the author or speaker actually had in mind. The phenomenon of resignification begins at the moment of original speech or reading. But the crucial observation is in the first instance of repetition. Why did members of the community reread or repeat what had once been said? The moment *relecture* (repetition) occurs the speech or literary work has a life of its own. It may in fact die early and not make it to canon. Its life may be relatively short as was probably the case for the sectarian literature discovered by archaeologists in modern times. Presumably such literature was meaningful for one denomination for a limited period of time. That is the religious literature, Jewish or Christian, which did not "make it" into the canon.

But the literature of the canon of an enduring community or communities is the Scripture that "made it." The nature of such literature is to be adaptable for life. Its adaptability is an intrinsic characteristic. The various enduring Jewish and Christian communities may disagree on the stability factor of the canon, what should be kept in and what should be left out, but all of them agree that Scripture is relevant or adaptable to the ongoing lives of those communities: it is canonical. Phyllis Trible has put it very well: "All scripture is a pilgrim wandering through history, engaging in new settings and ever refusing to be locked in the box of the past."[31] The Bible as canon reaches its full stature in the ongoing believing communities, the heirs of those communities which shaped it and passed it on in the first place. The danger to this point in the

31. In *ANQ* 11 (1971): 74.

modern history of biblical criticism has been to decanonize the Bible. It is time to recognize its true nature, in addition to recognizing its historical value.

There is a distinction to be made between what may be said historically about Scripture and what should be said canonically about it.[32] History and canon are not coextensive terms. Something may be canonically true without having been historically true. The Gospel of Matthew, for instance, precedes that of Mark canonically but not historically. The Pauline epistles follow the gospels and the Acts of the Apostles canonically, but preceded them historically. Recently, therefore, the bias for reconstructed history of formation of biblical literature has led some scholars to write introductions to the Bible putting the books thereof in their historical or chronological order rather than in the order in which the early communities transmitted them.[33] While it is true that the earliest manuscripts of the NT vary to a limited extent in the order of the placement of the gospels, they all put the gospels before Paul's letters. And while early manuscripts of the OT vary in ordering the Prophets, and certainly the *Ketubim* (Hagiographa or Writings), they all put the Torah first. To publish an introduction to either Testament that follows what biblical historical criticism has concluded is the chronological order of that testament may supply a historical perspective on the development of that literature and of certain ideas (e.g., the development of Christology). Or it may not. However, the perspective of the interrelationship of the literature within the Testament which the early communities saw may be lost.

The effort to relate biblical literature historically occurred rather early. Early Christian lists and manuscripts of the LXX, the OT of the early churches, place the Book of Ruth after the Book of Judges in an apparent effort to put it in some kind of historical order. No Jewish list or manuscript does so: in these Ruth always appears in the *Ketubim* along with the four other scrolls (Song of Songs, Ecclesiastes, Lamentations, and Esther). At an early stage each of the scrolls was associated with a calendar event in the Jewish year, and they were associated with each other in canonical ordering. It makes a difference how one views and reads Ruth, whether it is associated with the Book of Judges or with other literature relating to calendar feasts and fasts. Different sorts of

---

32. James Mays, "Historical and Canonical: Recent Discussions about the Old Testament and Christian Faith," in *Magnalia Dei*, 510–28.

33. Two examples are *The Jerome Biblical Commentary*, ed. R. E. Brown et al. (Englewood Cliffs, N.J.: Prentice-Hall, 1968) and Willi Marxsen, *Introduction to the New Testament* (Philadelphia: Fortress Press, 1968). See Helmut Koester (*Introduction to the New Testament*, 2 vols. [Philadelphia: Fortress Press, 1982]) for yet another approach.

questions arise out of the two distinct literary contexts. The same may be said for Esther which often, though not always, follows Ezra-Nehemiah in Christian manuscripts and lists but never in Jewish ones. At least there is traditional warrant for these variations.

In the case of modern introductions there is warrant for discussing biblical books in their alledged chronological order of composition. But there is also warrant for discussing them in their received canonical sequence. A different chemistry occurs. Canonical criticism says we should continue to honor what our ancestors in the faith had in mind as well as learn what we can from the results of the labors of biblical historical criticism.

We must also make a distinction between what is canonical and what was historical for theological reasons, that is, what the historian should say about ancient biblical views of God. It is one thing to say canonically that the Bible is a monotheizing literature, which it surely is. It is quite another to suggest that ancient Israel was a monotheizing people! On the contrary, even a cursory reading of the prophetic corpus indicates otherwise. They were apparently normal in their time and hence thought in basic, polytheistic terms. This is discernible also in the number of laws in the Torah which both expressly and indirectly prohibit polytheism. And it is clear from the "history" books as well, especially Joshua through Kings. The Yahwistic, monotheizing reformations of Asa, Hezekiah, and Josiah bear testimony to how pervasive and insidious in the human psyche the bent to polytheize really is. If truth be told, the human psyche has not changed in this regard but still finds it difficult to monotheize. It would seem to be our human lot to view reality in a fragmentary mode and to think of the cosmos as made up of irreconcilable warring factions, one or some of which must be defeated and destroyed for truth to prevail.

The Bible, in one perspective, may be viewed as the result of many efforts over some 1500 to 1800 years and through five different culture eras to monotheize over against a massive cultural backdrop of polytheism. Since it is clear that good, normal thinking Israelites were polytheizers for the most part, the remarkable thing is that the Bible as canon happens to be a monotheizing literature. In fact, this is its principal and basic hermeneutic shape. Not every portion of Scripture monotheizes as well as another. The idioms of its cultural frames are indeed used. How else could it have been? "Who is like thee among the gods, O Lord?" (Exod. 15:11). That liturgical and rhetorical question is at the very heart of the recitation of the *Shema'* in every Jewish worship service. It comes near the end of the blessings that follow the recitation. Does it detract from the first blessing before the *Shema*? "Blessed are you, O Lord our God, King of the universe, who form light and create darkness, who make peace and create all things." Hardly. In no way should light and darkness be viewed as symbols of Persian or other deities. On the contrary, over against that kind of polytheism the canonical God creates light and darkness, good and evil (Isa. 45:7).

Persian dualism was a cultural given in the postexilic period just as the earlier Bronze and Iron Age polytheistic idioms were used as in Exodus 15, the Song of the Sea. But Isaiah 45 and Exodus 15 should be seen as the results of struggles in different periods to monotheize over against the cultural givens. The fact that the cultural residues of the five different eras—Bronze Age, Iron Age, Persian, Hellenistic, and Roman—emerge in biblical speech is quite understandable. But they should be read not as subscribing to the supposed realities behind the idioms but rather as struggling to monotheize in the different settings over against those supposed realities. To monotheize is, in part, to engage in a resistance movement against a dominant mode of thinking whether in biblical antiquity or in the present.

It is just possible that the greatest challenge to the human psyche is the canonical mandate to monotheize. Most of ancient historical Israel failed at it most of the time, apparently, and most of Christianity has failed at it most of the time from the first century onward. It is advisedly called the First Commandment (cf. chapter 3 on canonical hermeneutics).

In distinguishing between the historical and the canonical, one is very close to the scholarly preoccupation with the reconstruction of historical moments and persons. One of the common results of biblical criticism in the late nineteenth and early twentieth centuries was to report that careful historical-critical study of the origins of biblical faith indicated that the biblical portrait of an event or person was not historically accurate. The patriarchs, Moses, Joshua, Jesus, and other biblical personages dear to the faith emerged looking sometimes quite different from their canonical portraits. For instance, it was suggested that the patriarchs in Genesis probably did not exist as human beings but may be actually humanized portraits of ancient minor deities in pagan pantheons. Abram means in Hebrew "exalted father," an epithet applied to several deities. The Genesis traditions would then have been making a tacit statement to the monotheizing effect that he had been no deity at all but was simply the founding father of the true faith. This tendency to humanize the gods of other peoples was a significant part of the monotheizing exercise of some of the biblical literature. Ishtar, it was said, was not a Mesopotamian goddess but simply the good, Jewish lass, Esther. Haman was not a Persian deity in actuality but simply a bad Persian leader under Xerxes. And Marduk was not a Babylonian god but Esther's nice, faithful Jewish uncle, Mordechai.

The reaction was soon forthcoming, and especially from the archaeological and philological schools of biblical interpretation. They were able to show how much closer together the historical and the canonical really were than what the German form critics had reported out of their literary and historical critical labors. Others joined them. The position was very attractive: solidly based historical reconstructions, that is, archaeologically and philologically based reconstructions of biblical history showed how accurate the Bible was for the most part. It was never said that history proved the faith: that was a caricature of the critics. What they did do, however, was to shed extrabiblical light on the biblical story, with the result that many of the faithful felt comforted that history had accounted for the accuracy of some of the major biblical accounts. And that had the result, for many conservative Jews and Christians, of speaking to the question of biblical authority.

Canonical criticism honors and incorporates the tools as well as the sound results of literary criticism, archaeology, and philology, especially where they assist in fleshing out the historical and sociological contexts of the ancient communities which shaped and were addressed by the biblical texts. But it serves to distinguish such tools and sound results from the role of such disciplines in addressing the questions pertaining to biblical authority. The latter do not properly fall within their competence. Canonical criticism can provide a bridge from the valid work of biblical criticism over to the necessary questions concerning the authority of Scripture in believing communities, both in antiquity and today.

III

Canonical Hermeneutics

The true shape of the Bible as canon consists of its unrecorded hermeneutics which lie between the lines of most of its literature.[1] Quests for canonical shape in the text itself or in its forms result repeatedly in observations about canonical pluralism. For almost every assertion one can find its contra-positive. The richness of the canon in this regard needs to be celebrated rather than ignored and denied as nearly all its adherents have tended to do. Conservatives deny it and liberals ignore it. Actually, it is one of the canon's most precious gifts that it contains its own self-corrective apparatus. No theological construct imposed on the Bible as canon escapes the scrutiny and critique of something else in it. Consistency is a mark of small minds. It can also be a manipulative tool in the hands of those who insist that the Bible is totally harmonious, and that they alone sing the tune!

One of the attitudes of nearly all students of the Bible is assuming that if they work hard enough and diligently enough in exegeting a passage they will eventually strike the "biblical" vein or core that anchors it to the rest of the Bible. Such an attitude has led to all kinds of falsehoods. This is especially the case with passages involving prophetic critique, whether in the prophetic corpus or outside it, as in the gospels or in Paul. And yet the tendency has been widespread. Surrendering that attitude could lead to a new day in biblical exegesis. Rhetorical hyperbole abounds in the Bible and should be released to speak its own word to the context for which it was a challenge, or to a similar context at a later point. Luke 14 says that those who considered themselves elect or invited would not taste the banquet, but Luke 15 says that the older brother, who made clear his belief that he was "entitled," was urged to attend that feast. Isaiah (2:4) and Micah (4:3) say that swords will turn to

1. James A. Sanders, s.v. "Hermeneutics," *IDB Sup;* "Hermeneutics in True and False Prophecy," in *Canon and Authority: Essays in Old Testament Religion and Theology,* ed. G. W. Coats and B. O. Long (Philadelphia: Fortress Press, 1977), 21–41; idem, *God Has a Story Too,* 1–27.

46

contradictions in Bible

plowshares and spears to pruninghooks, but Joel (3:10) commands that plowshares be turned to swords and pruninghooks to spears. Isaiah says, "Remember not the former things" (43:18) but also says, "Remember the former things of old" (46:9). Each spoke to or in a different context. Whenever I see a student get excited about Jeremiah and begin to see everything else in the Bible from that base, I insist he or she read Qohelet (Ecclesiastes). Qohelet does a Jeremiah on Jeremiah, so to speak. The one is prophetic critique, but so may the other be when the former is somehow generalized or absolutized. And for those who tend to absolutize the notion of justification by faith, I recommend a careful reading of the Pastoral Epistles.

But once the Bible's pluralism is sufficiently celebrated and valued, the question of the shape of the canon remains. Canonical criticism looks for that shape in the hermeneutics of the biblical authors and writers themselves. Biblical criticism has developed and refined the tools that permit us to ferret out those hermeneutics.

A major exercise in canonical criticism is locating and identifying two types of "precursor" material in the biblical passage being studied: the community traditions being called upon or reflected in the passage; and the international wisdom traditions being called upon or being reflected in the passage. In other words, one searches diligently for both the homegrown traditions and the borrowed ones. This is a first step in the canonical critical aspect of work on the passage after the exegete has defined the pericope by form-critical methods, done the text-critical work, and analyzed the structure of the passage.[2] This step employs some of the older methods of tradition history but goes considerably beyond it in that at this point the international wisdom traditions are as important as the national or the denominational ones. The next step is to discern the hermeneutics by which those identified traditions function in the passage, how they were adapted, represented, and resignified.

In the last fifty years the attitude toward what ancient Israel and early Christianity learned from others has changed considerably. Paul Tillich, for instance, once commented that while living in Dresden he hesitated each morning before reading the newspaper fearful that the archaeologists had found something more that would cause him to retreat another step in his faith. In his youth the pan-Babylonian school under Friedrich Delitzsch stressed how much the OT was indebted to ancient Babylon.

---

2. A different order of work in exegesis of a passage may be indicated by the peculiarities of the passage chosen. For a clear and excellent statement of how to exegete a biblical passage using the various subdisciplines of biblical criticism, now including canonical criticism, see Richard D. Weis, *A Handbook of Old Testament Exegesis*, unpublished, available through the author at P.O. Box 670, Claremont, Calif. 91711.

The hermeneutic behind such thinking was singularist, based upon a view of God as Redeemer of a particular group, who revealed truth to that group only. Tillich was probably reflecting the sensationalist articles appearing in the 1920s about King Tut and the tomb treasures which had been discovered only a short while before.

Today that attitude has changed considerably. Today whenever we learn that something else in the Bible was not homegrown but had been learned from others, such as the Babylonians or the Canaanites, we thank God for the Babylonians and Canaanites, and that ancient Israel had sense enough to learn from others of God's children. In other words, the newly perceived underlying hermeneutic is that of God as Creator of all peoples, as well as Redeemer in Israel and in Christ. Those are the two basic hermeneutic axioms operating in the Bible. Before turning to them, we need to define Wisdom in terms of that aspect of the exegetic exercise.

Wisdom pervades the Bible, but because of the way in which we use it, it may be seen as parallel to Israel's peculiar story and Christ's peculiar story, or the Gospel. Actually the two mingle frequently. Basically one thinks of Wisdom as that which passes over national borders and reaches deep into the common human experience. Many of the laws embedded in the Pentateuch were borrowed from the Babylonians, Assyrians, Egyptians, and Hittites—and probably by custom from the Canaanites. Most of the myths and legends that appear in the Bible were adapted by the biblical authors from foreign sources. Many proverbs and parables in the Bible are found elsewhere in the literatures of the eastern Mediterranean area.

Most of the preexilic laws embedded in the traditions called Jahwist and Elohist in the Torah were borrowed from neighbors. That is a simple fact which loses interest in and of itself. What is interesting is *how* the biblical authors adapted such laws. When such laws appear in the Pentateuch they signify quite a different hermeneutic shape. In the Code of Hammurabi the sun god Shamash is appealed to for authority, but it is the king himself who issues the laws as royal decrees. Not so in the Bible. There it is God who speaks directly through Moses to the people. God is as much the legislator as Moses is. In the Temple Scroll from Qumran, Moses is bypassed and God alone is legislator.

In noting *how* myths and other materials were adapted one makes similar observations. We know of five extant versions of the flood story related in the famous Gilgamesh Epic. Gilgamesh makes a journey to visit Utnapishtim to find out how he and Mrs. Utnapishtim came to be (semi-)divine and live immortal in the Far Distance at the Mouth of the

Two Rivers, a divine abode. They had built an ark and had survived the death-dealing waters of the flood. The similarities among the various flood stories at this point, including the biblical story in Genesis 6—9, are so striking that one needs to seek out where the differences lie, particularly in the biblical account.

That quest is indeed revealing. The accounts are closely parallel right up to the point of debarkation on dry land. There the biblical account begins to differ significantly. Noah and his family, and Utnapishtim and his, offer sacrifices. After that the biblical account differs remarkably! On the one hand, Mr. and Mrs. Utnapishtim are thereupon invited back on the deck of the ark, apotheosized by Ea, Enlil, and the other gods, and invited to live immortal in the Far Distance at the Mouth of the Two Rivers as their reward for riding out the flood. Noah, on the other hand, after being shown the rainbow and its promise and far from being given immortality, proceeds to a normal farmer's life, raises a vineyard, shames himself with his children, lives 950 years and dies! In fact, one then notes that Genesis 9 ends with the same refrain as the genealogies in Genesis 5: someone lived long years "and he died." Far from earning immortality by his obedience and good deeds, Noah ends up as mortal and sinful as everyone else; in fact, not totally unlike the sinful whose deeds, according to Genesis 6, brought on the flood in the first place!

Israel may have borrowed the story from her neighbors but it was the way in which she adapted it, the hermeneutics, that are important to note in any search for the shape of the canon. Pursuant to the general theme of Genesis 1—11, the flood story stresses the oneness of God over against the many gods and their jealousies in the other accounts; it stresses both the ethical and ontological integrity of God; and it relentlessly insists that only God is immortal. It is God who lives; it is all else that dies. God lives and gives life to whom he will. No one can earn it by good deeds. The flood story, when reviewed in this light, also seems to be more about God than about the flood. If there was a massive flood at some point in common human memory, shared in the wisdom literature of many peoples, the interest in it canonically is how God signified such disaster. The focus shifts ever so slightly away from the characters in the story to what God can do with them.

Hermeneutically, however, this is a *very* important shift. Ernst Fuchs and others have said that hermeneutics is theology and theology is hermeneutics. Canonically this means that it is one's view of God, or reality, which is axiomatic in how one reads a biblical passage. There is much left to do in pursuing canonical criticism, but inductive work in testing such observations indicates that in reading most passages it makes an immense difference whether one views God as the Redeemer God of a particular group or the Creator God of all people, or tries to hold the two views of God in mind together. If one has in mind God as Redeemer, it is almost inevitable that one will think of whom God redeemed and whether they can prove it, or whether they act like it. The focus becomes the characters in the story. If one has in mind God the Creator of all peoples, then one's interest is in what God was doing in the particular story and what God was doing and saying through it and the characters in it.

When I was a child growing up in Memphis I attended a Youth for Christ rally where a rather well-known Southern Baptist preacher, Robert G. Lee, was speaking. Someone asked him whether he thought Balaam's ass could talk. The questioner had apparently just read a book by Harry Emerson Fosdick who had said he did not believe Balaam's ass could talk. Lee's response was that if he had to choose between Balaam's ass and that man in New York as a preacher, he would certainly choose Balaam's ass. This memory has become a symbol for me of the modernist-fundamentalist controversy. Both were interested in the same thing, whether Balaam's ass could talk. The burning issue for both liberals and conservatives was the same: the focus for both was on the characters in the story rather than on God. The point of that pericope within the complex of Numbers 22—24 is not whether the ass could talk. If one reads such a passage on its own terms, and with the hermeneutics employed by the authors, then one's interest is on what she said! That is, what the text conveys. Moreover, the Balaam episode, when read in the light of the whole and on its own terms, clearly conveys the point that it is what the Lord puts in one's mouth that one must speak. The overall point of the Balaam story is that God can bless his people even through those whom their enemy employs to curse them. That God, or an angel, could speak through the ass also underscores the overriding point of the story—what God can do in and through the realities of life. It also makes the point that God's people should probably listen to outsiders, even their criticisms and oppositions: God might be sending a blessing.

Many such examples could be used to illustrate the point not only that hermeneutics make quite a difference in what a passage is allowed to convey but also that a canonical hermeneutic is axiomatically one's view of God while reading the text. The question of historical improbabilities, while not necessarily irrelevant, fades into the background.

Taking the Bible seriously on its own terms, by ferreting out the unrecorded hermeneutics which lie throughout its pages, has yielded five salient observations: One, the Bible is a monotheizing literature. Two, it betrays a broad theocentric hermeneutic. Three, much of it celebrates the theologem *errore hominum providentia divina* (God's grace works in and through human sinfulness). Four, in it God betrays a divine bias for the weak and dispossessed. Five, there is a fourfold hermeneutic process by which it adapted international wisdom.

The Bible is a monotheizing literature. The Bible probably should not be thought of as a monotheistic book but as a monotheizing literature. There is no serious treatise in it arguing monotheism philosophically. But every bit of it monotheizes—more or less well.

The Bible comes to us from five culture eras of struggles to monotheize over against different kinds of polytheism: the Bronze Age, the Iron Age, the Persian, Hellenistic, and Roman eras. Each of those cultures had its own kinds of polytheism, and the Bible reflects the various struggles to monotheize, that is, to pursue the Integrity of Reality. Each era left a residue of idioms derived from the polytheisms of its culture, precisely because of the struggle to monotheize. This can be seen especially well in those instances when Israel learned something from her neighbors, for then we can do a comparative study of the biblical and the nonbiblical material and discern precisely the hermeneutics of adaptation.

We can also discern such a hermeneutic by internal comparative studies. 2 Samuel 24 says that Yahweh induced David to take a census of the people and then that Yahweh punished him for doing so! That is monotheizing to the hilt, as it were. The same story in 1 Chronicles 21 says that the satan incited David to take the census and the Lord punished him for doing so. The chronicler is still monotheizing because the satan at that point was but a member of the heavenly council who could but do God's bidding. And yet the chronicler cannot be said to monotheize as completely as did the historian in 2 Samuel. Other such examples may show that the idioms of the various cultures through which the Bible passed or from which it is derived were indeed employed by the biblical authors of those times. Yet the burden of proof would fall on whoever might suggest that any biblical author or thinker polytheized. The principalities and powers and demons of the Hellenistic period show up in the NT as symbols of evil, disease, and disorder, but the burden of proof would fall on whoever might suggest that any NT author or thinker had ceased monotheizing and started polytheizing. Such idioms, like the characters in biblical stories, represent cultural conditioning and the condition of the created order, and should not be absolutized. The interest is in what God was doing in and through such cultural idioms and through such created beings. Luke 10:17-20 is an excellent case in point. Satan and demons are mentioned precisely to say God has total power over them and has given that power to Christ and his disciples.

The Bible is a monotheizing literature displaying the struggles of generations over some fifteen to eighteen centuries to pursue the Integrity of Reality. In this sense the Bible is a paradigm; it conjugates the nouns and verbs of the divine integrity in a plethora of different kinds of situations and conditions. To monotheize, in this sense, is not to progress or evolve toward monotheism, but rather to struggle within and against polytheistic contexts to affirm God's oneness, both in antiquity and today.

The Bible as canon betrays a broad theocentric hermeneutic. Canonical criticism locates and identifies whatever traditions are represented in a given passage and then attempts to discern the hermeneutics by which those traditions function in the text. So far the inductive work done by those of us pursuing canonical criticism is fairly consistent in showing a theocentric hermeneutic on the part of the biblical tradents. The interest was in what God was doing in and through the givens of the situation described and what God might do again. God is presented as Creator, Sustainer, Judge, Redeemer, and Re-creator. Insofar as we can discern, the interest was never anthropocentric or primarily sociological or political—not in the way the various accounts are presented canonically. The interest was in what God as Creator and Redeemer could do with the social conditions or the political situation. To moralize in reading a text is to focus on and even absolutize the cultural mores and conditions thereof. To theologize in reading a text is to focus on what God can do with the likes of the reader mirrored in the text. When biblical writers did moralize in theologizing it was more often than not to contrast what God had done with what Israel was doing, especially in prophetic critique.

Within the theocentric perspective the tradent may focus upon God as Israel's Redeemer God, or the redemptive work of God in Christ, and read the tradition as promise of God's grace. This usually issues in consolation and assurance that God is faithful to his promises. Or the tradent may focus on God as the Creator of all peoples and God of all creation and read the same tradition as challenge to Israel or church. The canonical prophets provide many illustrations of the latter. The point is well illustrated in those passages which record a debate or dispute between the canonical prophet, whose mission was to bring Israel's most precious traditions to bear as critique and challenge, and a contemporary colleague who interpreted the same precious traditions as comfort and encouragement.

There are two major hermeneutic axioms functioning in all such passages: that of prophetic critique when God as God of *all* is stressed; and that of a constitutive mode when God as particular Redeemer of Israel or church is stressed. Both are valid and legitimate and can be found throughout the Bible. The need of the people in their historical context and situation determines which is appropriate. The same Word of God which comforts the afflicted may also afflict the comfortable. The outside limits of choice as to which should apply would at least be that no such Word should ever be applied in order to make the cruel blind to their cruelty or to quench a dimly burning wick.

Much of the Bible celebrates the theologem: errore hominum providentia divina (God's grace works in and through human sinfulness). Abraham and Sarah may lie to save their skins (Gen. 12:11-13) and even laugh at God (Gen. 17:17 and 18:12-15), but these weaknesses do not stump God's purposes. The man of God from Judah may flunk the test of lifestyle—that is, personal obedience—but that in no way tarnishes the message he bears (1 Kings 13 and 2 Kings 23:17-18). The disciples may appear stupid, lethargic, self-centered, foolish and may even lie (Luke 22:1-62), but it is precisely in and through such earthen vessels that we have this treasure of truth called gospel.

One must not absolutize this observation, however. It apparently does not apply to most of the purely wisdom passages, such as proverbs and laws. One must not generalize this hermeneutic shape, as prevalent as it is in the Bible. One especially should not absolutize it; for against it one should place the lives of the prophets, for instance, whose messages were sometimes borne out by their peculiar lifestyles. The personal medium was sometimes the message: Isaiah's walking about Jerusalem naked for three years (20:3); Hosea's marital situation demonstrating God's own love for his errant people (chapters 1—3); both of them naming their children so as to communicate their messages (Isa. 7:3; 8:3; Hos. 1:4, 6; 2:1); Jeremiah's remaining celibate (16:2); Ezekiel's not mourning the death of his wife (24:16-18).

Nonetheless, the Bible frequently celebrates the theologem that human sinfulness is the stuff with which God works to effect his plan and do his work. God's grace is unearned and unmerited. Jacob was a scoundrel when God chose him to be Israel. Moses was a murderer and a fugitive from justice when God chose him to go back to Egypt to effect the liberation of his children and at Sinai to give them his will for their lifestyle. This is the hermeneutic of much of the Bible. As Martin Luther sharply claimed, God can carve the rotten wood or ride the lame horse.

The apostle Paul also noted that people might well moralize while reviewing such scriptural accounts and decide that sin was good to commit because God worked so well with it. Just after affirming that "where sin increased, grace abounded all the more," Paul checked the normal tendency to moralize that most people have always had in reading Scripture, by then asking, "Shall we sin the more that grace may the more abound? Absolutely not!" (Rom. 5:20—6:2). It is one thing to celebrate what God can do with the likes of us, as portrayed in the various biblical accounts of the situations of our biblical ancestors in the faith; it is quite another to follow their example. It is the example that God sets which we should follow. The imitation of God (*imitatio dei*) needs to be set in constant dynamic tension with human sinfulness (*errore hominum*). It is not that we can do what the accounts say God does, but it is abundantly clear that we should order our lives and conceive of programs of obedience in the light of these narratives of God's efforts to work with sinful humans like us.

God betrays a divine bias for the weak and dispossessed. Again, this hermeneutic should not be absolutized, but it is nonetheless pervasive. Like a real bias, it is not up for debate. "This man receives sinners and eats with them" (Luke 15:1) is not a peculiar trait of the NT Jesus. The trait there portrayed of the Christ is but a symbol of God's tendency to identify throughout the Bible with the poor and powerless. The fact that the God of the Bible exhibits such a bias is easily understood—historically, politically, and sociologically. Israel was located at the eastern end of the Mediterranean in an area that is a land bridge among three continents, truly a land flowing with milk and honey, rich in agriculture and minerals, endowed with enviable deep-water seaports and generally desirable to any government in the area that could raise surplus economy enough to field an army. Any country that could do so confronted Palestine. It was and is a highly desirable land. For this reason its inhabitants constantly have had to defend it or succumb to being a client state of powerful neighbors.

Israel was often defeated or overwhelmed by foreign forces. In fact, the whole of the Bible is largely shaped by the two devastating experiences of the destruction of Jerusalem, first in 587 B.C.E. and then in 69-70 C.E. People able to monotheize about those events and similar ones had to "go to the wall," and affirm God as the God of death as well as of life (1 Sam. 2:6). In this respect, the Bible largely presents a point of view on life "from down under."

But it is not only the national experience at large which figures here;

54

many if not most of the individuals who play important roles in God's story are not wealthy folks: Abraham had to go to Egypt to beg for food. There he nearly lost his wife with whom he bore the promise of the called people of God. Jacob had to work for the godless Laban for forty years. Joseph was sold as a slave by his own brothers. Moses was a fugitive.

One of the themes in the cycle of Elijah stories, as in others in the Bible, is the question of the identity of Israel. A historian would say that Ahab and Jezebel represented Israel as king and queen in Elijah's day. One ought not trust the historian who says otherwise. But 1 Kings 17 denies such reading and affirms that at this juncture in her history Israel was an old man—in the desert being fed by ravens or in a foreign land being sustained by a poor widow. The true Israel was not represented by her royalty but by a poor and powerless prophet. Themes such as the Suffering Servant in Isaiah or a man called Job, clobbered four times over, fit well into the story of Israel's struggle to monotheize in the middle of deprivation and suffering. Christ's own rejection, suffering, and passion are the epitome of the story in the Christian canon. In fact, this is such a pervasive theme that one is somewhat uncomfortable reading 1 Kings 10. "All King Solomon's drinking vessels were of gold, and all the vessels of the House of the Forest of Lebanon were of pure gold; none were of silver, it was not considered as anything in the days of Solomon" (10:21). Or, "the king made silver as common in Jerusalem as stones and cedars as numerous as the sycamores of the Shephelah" (10:27).

In 1 Kings 11, however, the Deuteronomic historian sorts it all out. The cultural and cultic needs of Solomon's seven hundred wives and three hundred assistant wives turned his head. "For Solomon went after Ashtoreth the goddess of the Sidonians and after Milcom the abomination of the Ammonites" (11:5). He polytheized! And that caused the split of the kingdom in the next generation and the reduction of his own to one tribe.

One of the clearest understandings of sin in the Bible is forgetting that everything is a gift of God. A persistent theme is that God's gifts cause people to forget God the giver and to think they possess something; they forget they are but stewards and trustees of whatever they have in life's brief passage from womb to tomb. In this sense, too, the Bible presents excellent human mirrors for modern readers to see themselves realistically. Abraham loved Isaac so much that he apparently forgot that his son was a gift of God. Sin is not something we can dismiss by obedience; it is also a human condition. Surely refusing to love Isaac would not have solved the problem. The only solution was the one presented, the tough recognition that Isaac, whom God had placed in Sarah's old, barren womb, was indeed God's gift, the next generation of the called folk of God (Genesis 22). This is a passage in which some of the best minds slip into moralizing. How can a good God ask Abraham to sacrifice his son? A question often asked. But to ask it is to polytheize. As though our God is by our standards a good God and there might be a bad one to do the things we don't like our God to do. To suggest that the solution is not to love anything, for everything is a gift, is to moralize without theologizing.

All humans in the Bible, save one, are shown as sinful. But it is a simple fact that the more of God's gifts one has, the more temptation there is to sin. It is only (theo)logical to say that it is more difficult for a rich person to attain unto the divine economy than for a camel to go through a needle's eye (Mark 10:25). They have more to be forgetful over! But God identifies with those who suffer real deprivation and poverty. The Bible goes so far as to suggest that God identifies with them. God was with Joseph in the pit and in prison in Egypt. He was with the Hebrew slaves in Egypt and the prisoners of war in Babylonian camps and prisons. And the Bible finally says that God crouched in the cradle of a baby Jew whose life was threatened by Herod's sword. He mounted the cross of one whose life had been crushed between the zealots and the establishment. He identified with neither group but with the victim who loved them both.

The hermeneutic process by which the wisdom of others was adapted and resignified. There was apparently a fourfold process: the ancient biblical thinkers depolytheized what they learned from others, monotheized it, Yahwized it, and then Israelitized it. I hasten to say that they did not fully engage in all four stages of the hermeneutic process. The flood story in Genesis is a prime example of how the first three are rather fully processed while the fourth was not at all engaged. That is, the biblical adapters, at whatever levels along the path of literary formation of Genesis 6—9, quite successfully depolytheized the story by ridding it entirely of mention of Ea, Enlil, or any of the other gods so prominent in the extra-biblical versions. Next they fully monotheized it by making abundantly clear that the one God alone was not only Creator but also Accuser, Judge, Redeemer, and the Promiser who would sustain and guarantee the promise. Next they Yahwized the story to a limited extent. Early efforts in source criticism made much of the fact that the proper divine name, Yahweh, appears in the Genesis flood account at places and the generic divine name, *'elohim*, at others. These, it was said, indicated a Yahwist and an Elohist, or Priestly source. Those source-critical hypotheses are being reviewed in numerous ways, and our work indicates they should be. But even if two or more sources are discerned in the account, for our purposes it is sufficient to observe that the Yahwizing did indeed take place to some extent.

But the biblical writers failed to Israelitize it. The ark lands not on Mount Zion, or even on Mount Zaphon, but on Ararat. The universal nature of the flood experience, as indicated in all the versions, may have suggested leaving the international dimension, just as the use of *'elohim*, by whatever source, may indicate the same.

That the fourfold process was not fully followed in all instances of borrowing and adaptation is to be expected. In antiquity the author was not conscious of the process: it is a tool we have developed by inductive work on the texts that suggest borrowing. The poignant story of God's testing Abraham (Genesis 22) by telling him to sacrifice Isaac had undoubtedly been a story derived from a culture or people where child sacrifice was practiced. The tension and value for that community would have resided in the fact that the priest who had to conduct the sacrifice was father to the child who was to be sacrificed, his only child! When Israel incorporated it into the story-line that begins with God's promise of progeny to Abraham and Sarah in Genesis 12, the above process was followed quite closely. It was clearly depolytheized of whatever gods were involved (e.g., Moloch). But more significantly, it was fully monotheized: the very God who had promised the progeny and had finally given Isaac through Sarah's old, barren womb when she was 90, now asked for him back. Abraham had loved Isaac so much he simply forgot his son was God's gift. Loving God's gift is a beautiful and wonderful thing and much to be desired; but lurking within it is the seed of idolatry, the displacement of the giver by love of the gift. All four aspects of the hermeneutic process of adaptation of this story into Israel's story of election and promise appear to have come into play: depolytheizing, monotheizing, Yahwizing, and Israelitizing.

The monotheizing step was and is the most challenging to the human mind. It seems at first repulsive to monotheize. How can a good God ask Abraham to sacrifice his son (Gen. 22:2)? How can God harden Pharaoh's heart (Exod. 9:12 et passim; Rom. 9:18)? How can Isaiah say that he had been commissioned by God to preach that the people's heart would be fat, their ears heavy, and their eyes closed lest they repent and be healed (Isa. 6:10)? How can God be a holy warrior at the head of enemy troops battling his own people (Isa. 28:21)? How could Christ's crucifixion be in the "definite plan and foreknowledge of God" (Acts 2:23)? This is the stuff of which monotheizing is made. It is not easy for the human psyche to grasp. It is indeed the first commandment, not only of the ten (Exod. 20:2-3; Deut. 5:6-7) but of the Bible as canon. It emerges through all its pages as the greatest challenge, perhaps, of all it brings to the human condition.

How are we to pursue the Integrity of Reality, this oneness of God, when it often *seems* to go against the grain of all that is decent and good? It is the first article of faith, for there is no evidence we can cull inductively by science or experience to support it. All human experience is no more valuable than that of the three blind folk around the elephant, when it comes to Reality. Is the universe ever exploding outward? Did it start with a bang? How can that we all would call evil be an integral part of that Reality, Dietrich Bonhoeffer's term for God? And yet the Bible insists that there is no amount of evil which God cannot redeem and resignify. Even when jealous brothers sell Joseph into slavery? Even when Pharaoh says to Moses, "Hold on; you're moving too fast"? Even when massive armies threaten the very extinction of God's people? Even when his Son so offends and so loves both the zealots and the establishment of first-century Palestine that he is crushed between opposing visions of what was right for society at that time?

Paul the apostle, who monotheized consistently in his reading of Scripture for his churches and pursued a theocentric hermeneutic in working out his understandings of Christology and ecclesiology, tackled the monotheizing challenge directly and did not evade it. "For the scripture says to Pharaoh, 'I have raised you up for the very purpose of showing my power in you, so that my name may be proclaimed in all the earth.' So then he has mercy upon whomever he wills, and he hardens the heart of whomever he wills" (Rom. 9:17-18). As the OT writers and thinkers, so the contributors to the NT monotheized more or less well, yet they all monotheized. But Christians have rarely, since NT times, done so at all. A few—Augustine, Anselm, Calvin, the Niebuhrs, and others—have struggled to do so. But most of us collapse with the effort. It is so much easier, apparently, to let members of the heavenly council, such as the satan, rival God and be a successful rebel at that! It is seemingly easier to fragmentize truth.

And yet we must monotheize if we are to meet the canonical challenge *par excellence.* Abraham's forgetting that Isaac was God's gift was normal precisely because he loved Isaac so much. Every generation of

58

the called people of God is a gift of God. We Christians forget that Christ, the Son of God, was God's gift to the world, and tend to make Christ an idol and a symbol of divisiveness in humanity. Christomonism is Christianity's failure to monotheize. I speak not only of some good lay folk who apparently think that there are three in heaven awaiting a fourth to play bridge. I speak of some well-trained scholars and theologians who simply collapse with the effort to meet the challenge. Just as the heavenly council was a result of ancient Israel's effort to monotheize over against foreign pantheons of the Iron Age, so the trinitarian formula was a result of early Christianity's brave efforts to monotheize in the Hellenistic-Roman period.[3] But some Christians easily slip into thinking that the triune God is three gods. To adapt to the surrounding forms of polytheism in order to express in the idioms of those times the struggle to monotheize is normal. The Bible speaks in the cultural idioms of the five culture eras through which it passed, of necessity, because the writers and their hearers lived in those times and idioms. But this does not permit us to absolutize the idioms—either the heavenly council idiom to deny there was a pantheon, or the trinitarian idiom to deny Hellenistic polytheism. The fact that the early churches made a doctrine of the trinitarian formula did to a degree absolutize it, that is, freeze the idiom for all time. That has been both good and bad. Good, because an integral part of the doctrine is the insistence on the one God though expressed in three persons. Bad, because Christians have tended (a) to slip into polytheism because of the formula and (b) to think that Christ revealed God rather than God's continuing his self-revelation in Christ fully and completely. God is the subject of all the verbs of the Torah-Christ story.

As to the Exodus, one only needs to think it through. What if Pharaoh had been softhearted? What if he had invited Moses into the palace after the first demonstration and offered to write up an emancipation proclamation? "Go ahead, Moses, pull the rug out from under the whole economy; go with my blessing." There might have been a monument of stones erected near Goshen in gratitude to Pharaoh for archaeologists to discover, but there would have been no Torah. The reason my own church split asunder in 1861 was that many good, faithful, sincere Presbyterians in the South accused their northern communicants of meddling in politics—abolitionism. It has taken us 122 years to mend that rift, and we fail to understand why Pharaoh's heart was hard (from the Hebrews' standpoint, of course)?! What we really do not like,

---

3. See the still stimulating treatise by my late, beloved colleague, Cyril C. Richardson, *The Doctrine of the Trinity* (Nashville: Abingdon Press, 1958).

perhaps, is the statement in Exod. 9:12 and elsewhere that God hardened Pharaoh's heart. We do not want our nice, good God involved in politics either. Of course, God is not a puppeteer. Such passages must be read in light of the perception of God that emerges from the full canon. God is indeed sovereign; but God is not a chess player. Far from it, God grants humans full freedom of will. What the Bible as canon asserts is that there is no amount of evil, or hurt, or suffering we experience or create which is beyond the reach of God to redeem. He is still sovereign even when we, like Pharaoh, refuse to share our power.

Each generation must ask in its own way the central question of faith. Have we placed ourselves beyond the reach of God to redeem? As noted earlier, we live between the pride of idolatrous humanism and the fear of the mushroom cloud—both products of the Enlightenment. "I have set my bow in the cloud" (Gen. 9:13). We seem to have sight enough to see clearly the cloud, but not vision enough to see God's bow in it. We might regain the vision Scripture offers if while reading it we would attempt to meet its foremost challenge—to monotheize.

IV

Work to Do

Canonical criticism is only about a decade old. While it had precursors in the 1960s, 1972 seems to mark its inception.[1] Much progress has been made, but much remains to be done, especially further inductive searches. Just as the history of transmission of the text of the OT has recently been rewritten, so the history of the canonical process needs now to receive careful attention.[2] Early efforts have been made for both Testaments, but the work should continue with more attention paid to the problem of closure of canon, though that may need to await other work.

There need to be many more diachronic and, where pertinent, synchronic studies of function of canonical traditions, figures, ideas, and texts.[3] This is perhaps the most urgent task. The method of comparative midrash is in place and is the major tool for use in these studies, along with the triangle (see Appendix). The triangle is important so that the historical and sociological context (bottom right angle) in which a tradition or text (bottom left angle) is called upon may be as clear and full as available data allow, and so that the hermeneutics (top angle), by which the tradition or text functions, may be as clearly identified as possible. No history of function of tradition or text can now be valid and fully valuable until each of the three essential factors (points of the triangle) is seen in relation to the others: tradition or text, historical and sociological context, and hermeneutics.

From such inductive labor should emerge a permissible hermeneutic range that indicates what is hermeneutically fair, according to the canonical process, to use in the believing communities today in re-

---

1. See chap. 1, n. 33.
2. See chap. 1, n. 26.
3. Some examples to date: James A. Sanders, "Habakkuk in Qumran, Paul and the Old Testament," *JR* 39 (1959): 232–44; idem, "From Isaiah 61 to Luke 4," in *Christianity, Judaism and Other Greco-Roman Cults*, ed. Jacob Neusner (Leiden: E.J. Brill, 1975), 1: 75–106; Geza Vermes, *Scripture and Tradition*, 2d ed. (Leiden: E.J. Brill, 1973). See n. 5 below.

presenting and resignifying a biblical tradition or text to address new problems. For instance, since there is so amazingly little allegory used by *biblical* tradents (distinct from postbiblical expositors), it may be that we should decide that use of allegory today is suspect and violates the inherent constraints within canonical texts. It should be noted that much of what has been called allegory in the Bible is really either typology (e.g., the Epistle to the Hebrews) or simply analogy (e.g., the parable of the sower). The Book of Revelation especially needs scrutiny as to the hermeneutics of its author(s) when re-presenting canonical traditions. Paul's designated allegory in Gal. 4:21-26 is without question an allegorical hermeneutic (besides being constitutive). But one wonders if true allegorical interpretation is not rare, at least in the Western canons, and if it needs to be located and identified carefully and perhaps eventually circumscribed in usage today. It certainly needs controls, and further work may indicate what the controls should be.

The quest for the unrecorded hermeneutics that lie between the lines of Scripture needs to continue apace. If we do not moralize upon first reading these texts but theologize in order to hear what God does, and if we avoid absolutizing the customs and ethics of antiquity, then we may discover that biblical hermeneutics are as canonical, if not more so, than all the cultural givens they adapt and interpret. It may be that the energy of the struggles of our ancestors in the faith to pursue the Integrity of Reality is the most precious heritage the canon has to offer. We today have no need to fight the same kinds of polytheism that they fought: focusing on ancient polytheisms and falsehood may but blind us to our own. In short, to monotheize may not be the only commandment in the Bible, but it is the first in the sense that everything else derives from it.

A necessary task, barely begun, is that of analyzing the structure of whole biblical books or larger literary units. A recent dissertation done at Claremont, supervised by Rolf Knierim, provides a brilliant structure analysis of the whole of the book of Isaiah. Marvin Sweeney, probably for the first time since the rise of biblical critical scholarship, has outlined the sixty-six chapters of Isaiah using all the tools of critical scholarship, and especially the tool of structure analysis which Knierim has developed in his form-critical work on the OT.[4] The function of the various sections of the book, which scholarship has long since identified as coming from various hands at various times, is now seen in context of the whole. The School of Isaiah at some point put together a poignant statement of its understanding of what God had done in letting Assyria

---

4. See Marvin Sweeney entry in n. 5 below.

and Babylonia punish and purge his people so that they could be a teacher of righteousness to all God's world. Peoples would flow eventually to Zion, a totally resignified Zion, not as to a world power but to learn Torah. Israel's real abiding authority and identity is that of God's teacher to all his creation. Within the larger canonical frame, then, Isaiah's statement would function to show God's purposes for his cosmos as its Creator and eventual Redeemer through the agency of an elect teacher, a teacher sorely chastened and disciplined but trained in a hermeneutic depth sufficient to the vocation.

Another important task will be that of establishing a canonically permissible range of resignification. As concepts, figures, and texts journey through the Bible from inception through the last books of the NT, they become resignified to some extent. The crucial question has to do with the limits to which the readjustments in meaning canonically may go. Some work has been done,[5] but much more is in order before we are anywhere near making a sound judgment.

A rich area for work in this regard is the central, or "Travel Section," of Luke's gospel (9:51—18:14). The sequential pericopes of that section are ordered from beginning to end by Greek word-tallies with sequential passages in Deuteronomy 1—26.[6] The question is how far the resignification goes. The Mary-Martha pericope in Luke 10:38-42 lies opposite Deut. 8:1-10. Mary is practically an illustration of the Deuteronomic point that no person (*anthropos*) lives by bread alone but by everything that proceeds out of the mouth of the Lord (Deut. 8:3). There is hardly any resignification at all so that one might place Luke 10:38-42, on a scale of one to ten, right at one.

The eschatological banquet in Luke 14:7-24 lies opposite the Holy War legislation in Deuteronomy 20. The excuses one may offer to claim exemption in a Holy War become the reasons the elect or invited (*keklemenoi*) in Luke decline the summons to the banquet. They knew that the victory banquet which followed the battle of Holy War was for

5. Dissertations done by my students in the field include: Merrill P. Miller, *Scripture and Parable: A Study of the Function of the Biblical Features in the Parable of the Wicked Husbandman and Their Place in the History of Tradition* (1974); Paul E. Dinter, *The Remnant of Israel and the Stone of Stumbling in Zion According to Paul (Romans 9—11)* (1979); Wm. Thomas Miller, *Early Jewish and Christian Hermeneutic of Genesis 18:1-16 and 32:23-33* (1979); Mary Howard Calloway, *Sing, Oh Barren One* (1979); Jane Schaberg, *The Father, The Son and the Holy Spirit: The Triadic Phrase in Matthew 28:19b* (1980: Chico, Calif.: Scholars Press, 1982); Sharon H. Ringe, *The Jubilee Proclamation in the Ministry and Teaching of Jesus: A Tradition-Critical Study in the Synoptic Gospels and Acts* (1980); Craig Evans, *Isaiah 6:9-10 in Early Jewish and Christian Interpretation* (1983); Marvin Sweeney, *Isaiah 1—4 and the Post-Exilic Understanding of the Isaianic Tradition* (1983). See also the excellent study by Phyllis Trible, "Journey of a Metaphor," in *God and the Rhetoric of Sexuality* (Philadelphia: Fortress Press, 1978), 31-59.

6. C. F. Evans, "The Central Section of St. Luke's Gospel," in *Studies in the Gospels*, ed. D. E. Nineham (Oxford: Blackwell, 1955), 37-53; James A. Sanders, "The Ethic of Election in Luke's Great Banquet Parable," in *Essays in Old Testament Ethics* (J. Philip Hyatt, In Memoriam), ed. J. L. Crenshaw and J. T. Willis (New York: KTAV, 1974), 245-71.

the victors, but since they wanted and needed to show belief that as Holy Warrior God did not need many soldiers on the field of battle (a principal factor in Holy War tradition in the Bible), they would sacrifice coming to the banquet to follow. In the parable the master waxes angry with that response and summons the "obviously undeserving" (from the standpoint of the *keklemenoi*) to fill the banquet hall. Here a big shift has taken place in that, pursuant to a major theme in Luke's gospel, the elect (*keklemenoi*) just had not come to accept the messianic fact that with Christ the great Jubilee had been introduced. The "big Sabbath," in which the historic laws about the Sabbath and nearly all other legislation would be set aside, had been introduced. The battle in the banquet parable in Luke 14, in other words, is seen already to have taken place: the Jubilee in Christ had begun. It was indeed time for the victory banquet. But those who could not believe, or had not heard, that the eschatological Jubilee had begun could not believe that this banquet was for all. Not only those who had not fought the battle (God was doing that in Christ) but even the poor, the maimed, the blind, and the lame would be invited to celebrate this victory. And these were the very ones the Essenes at Qumran would not permit anywhere near either the final battle field or the sacred meal, the proleptic messianic banquet.[7] This resignification of the Holy War legislation in Deuteronomy is considerable. The hermeneutic function in Luke 14 is one of eschatological prophetic critique. The Holy War legislation has been caught up into a whole different world, that of the eschatologically introduced Jubilee. One would have to put this at about eight or nine on a resignification scale of one to ten.

The parable of the two sons in Luke 15:11-32 lies opposite the legislation in Deut. 21:18-21 about the stubborn and rebellious son who becomes a glutton and a drunkard. The law provides that if the son refuses to repent he may be brought to court and sentenced to death by stoning. The Lukan parable gives a beautiful illustration of the case where the son does indeed seek reconciliation, as the law, of course, allows. What might happen, the parable says, if the son repents? And it is, of course, a stirring statement about the depth of the grace of the Father in forgiveness when the son returns. The law would allow for all the rejoicing of which the family was capable in that instance. And so the parable, like the two preceding in the same chapter, ends on a lesson for the faithful, those who do not get themselves lost, that the grace of God is unmerited and cannot be earned by any amount of obedience. The

7. Sanders, "The Ethic of Election," esp. 261-66.

continuity-of-generational-values-legislation in Deuteronomy has been used by Luke's Jesus to give a lesson on divine grace. It has, indeed, been considerably resignified; but it has in no way been violated. Because of the repentance, the focus was shifted from the rebellion of the one child to the love of the parent, and then finally to the rebellion of the other child who had "needed no repentance." This would have to be put at about seven on such a scale, for the parable in no way contradicts the legislation. The eschatological framework of Luke, while present, is not quite as prominent here as in the parable in Luke 14.

The parable of the two men who go up to the temple to pray in Luke 18:9-14 lies opposite Deut. 26:1-15. Chapter 26 is the last in the legal section of Deuteronomy and is the climax not only of that section but of the book. In fact, because of the final literary form of the Pentateuch as a whole, the chapter provides a fitting climax to Torah. It is part of Moses' last will and testament.

In Deuteronomy 26 Moses tells the gathered assembly what they should do after they have crossed into Canaan and come to that place where God is to be worshipped. They should engage in a service of thanksgiving for which Moses provides them both a confession of faith *and a confession of obedience*. The latter occurs in 26:12-15 and is generally overlooked in dealing with this chapter. The first confession, that of identity and faith (26:5-10), Gerhard von Rad called Israel's *credo*.[8] While that may not be so, there are nonetheless two confessions, the second one a confession of obedience. We are not accustomed to confessions of obedience, but Israel had them (see Job 29), and Luke knew that. Of the two men in the parable who go up to the temple to pray, the Pharisee engages in a prayer of thanksgiving, a confession of faith, and then one of obedience, as Moses commanded.

The problem with confessions of obedience, useful as they may be to induce people to attempt to lead lives of obedience, is that they can easily lead to bragging. Philips Brookes could apparently say, upon seeing a wretched soul, "There but for the grace of God go I." But in the mouth of another that could easily sound like bragging. To say one is gifted was originally a statement of humility: God gave me this talent, I did not create it. But the phrase today, "I am gifted," becomes a statement of pride. The Pharisee confessed that he had tried to obey the law. As the wise teacher points out, however, the confession of obedience even with the best of people can become a statement of pride; better was the simple confession of sin and plea for mercy from

8. See chap. 2, n. 8.

the hated tax collector. This parable, like the one in Luke 15, took the law and showed another side of it: what if the rebellious and cantakerous son repents? What if the confession of obedience leads one to bragging about one's righteousness? Both parables stress that God's grace is totally unearned and unmerited—a point Deuteronomy itself stressed (Deut. 9:4ff. et passim). One might judge the resignification at about four or five on a scale of ten.

The hermeneutics employed in all these cases is that of understanding God as Creator as well as Redeemer. They stress God's freedom as Creator and God's grace as Redeemer. Each contains a surprise, some measure of prophetic critique for those who are confident they are among God's elect.

It is comparatively simple to study Luke in this regard since he used a Greek translation of the OT and, as a former Gentile converted to Christianity did not, like Matthew and Paul, remember targumic or midrashic interpretations of the OT passages he cited or to which he alluded. In the case of those writings, as well as of John in some cases, one often needs to be aware of some intermediate Jewish interpretation of the Scripture passage cited, or allusion.

A good case in point is Matthew's great supper parable, vaguely parallel to Luke's (14:7-24). The feast in Matthew 22 is a wedding feast (*gamos*) in contrast to Luke's banquet (*deipnon*). Furthermore, to understand fully the Matthean parable one needs to know the targum to the sacrifice and feast described in Zeph. 1:7-9.[9] There is a great deal to be done in this regard.

Every passage of Scripture of any substance can be read in at least two different ways, depending on whether it is read by the constitutive mode or the prophetic. This difference is easy to illustrate with many passages, such as a seemingly difficult one, John 14:7. "No one comes to the Father but by me." Here I will bracket discussions of the original meanings of the sentence in and for early Johannine communities which might have been tempted by gnostic modes of thought. By the constitutive mode this passage can be read as quite exclusivist: our Christ is the only path to God. In fact, reading the Bible exclusively in the constitutive mode can issue in a totally denominational, if not tribal, reading of the whole Bible. Christian inability to monotheize has frequently resulted in tribalization both of Christianity and of the Bible, just as modern political Zionism has resulted in many people secularizing and nationalizing the Hebrew Bible. Both issue from exclusively constitutive

9. J. Duncan M. Derrett, "The Parable of the Great Supper," in *Law in the New Testament* (London: Darton, Longman and Todd, 1970), 126-55, esp. 126-29.

modes of reading. Too narrow a reading of John 14:7 can, of course, be challenged by setting it beside John 10:16, "I have sheep not of this fold."

But John 14:7 can be read differently when seen by the hermeneutic mode of prophetic critique. An Amos, a Jeremiah, or a Jesus could take this seemingly exclusivist verse and read it so as to challenge those who would cite it to support their own position. Such a reading would show that those who make such claims have misunderstood considerably the meaning of Christ, even in John, and certainly the Christ that emerges from the canon as a whole. Their perception of Christ is self-serving and canonically false. It is they who have missed the Christ path. The Christ path to God that emerges canonically celebrates the freedom of the God of grace to express that grace in ways quite shocking to exclusivists who claim to have the only right way to read these texts—theirs!

Further work needs to be done in order to find, if possible, a biblical passage of substance which absolutely can be read in only one way and cannot possibly be read differently by the two hermeneutic modes. The choice of which reading is canonically appropriate would be determined by discerning the needs of the congregation or audience addressed. It is as important to exegete the context to be addressed as it is to exegete the text to be read.[10]

Canonical criticism not only looks for all the traditions, texts, and precursors that flow into a passage studied but it also seeks to determine exactly how that tradition functioned in the text and the hermeneutics by which it did so. The tools by which it does so are comparative midrash with the triangle (see Appendix) always in mind. The range of resignification that canonical criticism eventually hopes to identify within the canonical orbit should provide limits and guidelines for modern interpreters and tradents who today will "go and do likewise" in their sermons, lessons, commentaries, and the like. Since a certain amount of resignification takes place every time a passage is read afresh, canonical criticism may eventually be able to provide fair rules for resignification and hence controls for what goes on all the time anyway. Thereby, one would be more responsible to current believing communities than simply regretting what is natural and what has been going on literarily since the earliest of biblical times, insisting somehow that only original meanings are permissible.

The question most often asked in relation to seeing the Bible as canon is whether more literature can be added. Canonical criticism responds to

10. The prophet Ezekiel (33:23-29) utterly rejects, in his day, 586 B.C.E., an interpretation or application of a divine promise to Abraham which nearly fifty years later, 540 B.C.E., Isaiah of the exile advances as gospel (Isa. 51:1-3). See chap. 3, n. 1.

the question in a way different from the way in which it is usually asked. If the very nature of canon is viewed as a paradigm of previous believing communities' struggles in their contexts with the issues of faith, rather than as a box of jewels of wisdom forever negotiable, then nothing need be added. The canonical paradigm shows how believing communities may learn to hear the voice of God from outside the inner community traditions. The Bible as canon is a veritable textbook of hermeneutics on how to adopt and adapt wisdom from any part of God's creation.

Epilogue

Clergy and Laity

What does all this mean for the ways in which pastors and lay folk can read the Bible today? What can be learned from the hermeneutics the biblical authors used for reading what they themselves wrote? The way they read what was authoritative or Scripture for them ought to say something about the way we ought to read what they wrote. How can we go about reading the Bible on its own terms?

Canonical criticism, for the Christian, sees the Bible in terms of Scripture, not primarily in terms of testaments. It seeks the lines of continuity as well as of discontinuity within Scripture. It is wary of generalizing or of absolutizing any of the cultural givens or idioms through which these traditions have passed in the some 1500 to 1800 years of their formation. The NT in this sense, for the Christian, is also biblical! The Jewish canon is the shortest of all, and yet most Jews view it through the prism of the kinds of ethical monotheism evident in Mishnah, Talmud, and the Responsa. Hellenism has influenced them significantly, as Saul Lieberman and others have shown.[1] The Jewish perspective on canon is not totally dissimilar from the Christian, except that perhaps Judaism may find it even more difficult to theologize on first reading biblical texts than Christians, for whom it is difficult enough. Moralizing has its place, but not upon *first* reading most of these texts.

Scripture has its proper *Sitz im Leben* in the believing communities which are today's heirs of those who formed and shaped it in antiquity. There is where it reaches its full stature. The Bible is a precious source for reconstructing history, but that is not its primary, or canonical, function.

Scripture is not so much a treasury of wisdom from antiquity, as it is primarily a paradigm provided by our ancestors in the faith for ways to

1. See Saul Lieberman, *Hellenism in Jewish Palestine* (New York: Jewish Theological Seminary, 1962).

69

decline the nouns and conjugate the verbs of God's creation of and redemption of his world. It is also a paradigm for ways to decline and conjugate the nouns and verbs of believers in any generation who are called to pursue the Integrity of Reality. It is a paradigm on ways to monotheize and to narrate the current episodes of the ongoing story of creation and redemption, and on ways to prepare for that eschaton when the story will culminate in the fullness of that integrity.

There are two basic hermeneutic axioms used by the biblical authors, speakers, and tradents, both OT and NT: *the constitutive* and *the prophetic*. These stem from the two fundamental views of God: the Creator of all things and peoples, and the Redeemer in Israel and in Christ. They work together always, but one receives more emphasis than the other in re-presenting canonical traditions, according to the discerned needs of those addressed. In the case of *prophetic critique*, those needs are probably quite different from the ones which the people think they need. When the tradent thought primarily of God as God of all peoples as well as the Redeemer God, the hermeneutic at play was that of prophetic critique, God judging his own people. This critique developed in all probability out of the community (Torah story) traditions being re-read through the prism of international wisdom in which God is clearly seen as the God of all. When the tradent thought primarily of God as the Redeemer God of a peculiar people, Jewish or Christian, as well as the Creator God, then the hermeneutic at play was *constitutive,* God saving and comforting his own people. The one emphasizes the freedom of the God of grace; while the second emphasizes the freedom of the grace of God. Analysis of the book of Isaiah shows that the distinction here was not between the so-called Mosaic and Davidic theologies but between these two hermeneutic axioms, whether used to interpret the Mosaic or the Davidic. The prophet Isaiah is a prime example of the application of prophetic critique to Davidic traditions.

The hermeneutic techniques and rules most often seen in the Bible are those related to historical typology, in which a story of what God had done before was reviewed to gain light as to what God might do in the new situation. The aspect of the story reviewed was re-presented, made new again, by reading or reciting it in the new context.

A major hermeneutic dimension here is memory, or *anamnesis*, in which both time and space are transcended in re-*present*ing the old story. Another major hermeneutic dimension here is that of dynamic analogy.

By *dynamic analogy* we mean re-presenting the tradition, consciously identifying with the character or characters in the tradition most representative of the new hearers or readers. This hermeneutic move presupposes the view that believing communities are essentially pilgrim folk always needing the canonical challenge to move on and take another step on the pilgrimage toward the goal God's story or history envisages. Modern Christians and Jews would by this dimension identify with their counterparts addressed in the tradition, that is, not with Joseph, Jeremiah, or Jesus, but with those around them who heard their challenges. To read the Joseph story, identifying with his brothers rather than with Joseph, renders a totally different story than if one identifies with Joseph. Most all faithful Christians, who are trying to lead obedient lives, should identify in the NT with the good, faithful Pharisees, or Sadducees, or Essenes, or indeed with the good, responsible Romans, *not* with Jesus, in order for the dimension of *dynamic analogy* to bring out the challenge Jesus leveled against his fellow religious Jews, as well as the Romans who bore the burden of being a world power.

Dynamic analogy also means identifying with different characters in the accounts, and not always with the same ones, each time read. In the parable of the hundred sheep in Luke 15, one may identify with the lost sheep, which most people probably do without thinking about it; or with the shepherd, which many pastors and teachers may do; or with the ninety-nine faithful who were left in the wilderness exposed to preying animals and the elements, while the shepherd left them looking for the sheep that wandered off. We really learn the meaning of grace then!

In reading of Saul's conversion in Acts 9 (or 22 or 26) we may identify with Saul, as most people probably do, without thinking about it; or with Ananias, who had the courage to call his enemy brother; or with the congregation in Damascus threatened by Saul's inquisitional campaign against young Christian churches. Where were they when Ananias took his heart in hand and obeyed *his* vision of the Christ? Different points and messages may be heard by simply being conscious of whom, or what, one identifies with in reading biblical accounts and stories.

If one reads the Bible as a paradigm, rather than as a casket of jewels of wisdom, there are *four canonical perspectives* to keep in mind. The *first* is that of the "ambiguity of reality" from the point of view of humans in any situation. God as Integrity of Reality is the object of faith, derived from the vision which the Bible as canon offers the faithful as its principal gift. The ambiguity of reality is where we all live. Someone has said that, should God come on earth with all the credentials heaven could afford, there would still be a debate about God's identity. Every coin of any value whatever has two sides. Every bullet has two names. There is no such thing as a victory without a defeat—on this side of the eschaton. Terrorists are called freedom fighters by some. All the "patriots" in the American Revolution were guilty of acts of treason according to British law. The ambiguity of reality is where we live.

Neither history nor theology can be based on a hermeneutic of "good guys and bad guys"; and yet most people still read the Bible in that way. If we keep in mind that God is the God of all, as well as Redeemer in Israel and in Christ, then it might be possible to identify with Raamses, Nebuchadnezzar, Herod, and Pilate on occasion and hear what the texts, where they appear, say to us then. They were God's human beings, too. We learn to admit our own betrayals of Christ and come to be grateful that Judas Iscariot, apparently a very dedicated young zealot who wanted Rome to go home, was also at the table and received the bread and the cup. Exodus says God hardened the heart of Pharaoh, and the NT says that satan entered into Judas Iscariot (Luke 22:3). But satan was not a rival god; to think so is polytheizing. From our point of view, would we have preferred Judas to be a young hero who helped save Jesus from crucifixion? But then we would have no gospel, just as we would have no Torah had Pharaoh instead of God issued the emancipation proclamation.

The Bible deals in realism. It does not clean up the human situation, at least not much. Chronicles started to do so, for moralizing had reared its head by the fifth century B.C.E.; even so, Chronicles does not erase the sinfulness of the human situation. The Bible is highly realistic; and this is surely one of the reasons it became canon, that is, adaptable for life to all generations to come. It mirrors reality and offers a vision of integrity.

The *second* paradigmatic canonical perspective is the one that requires us to read biblical texts as mirrors for identity, not as models for morality. Like Nathan's court case in 2 Samuel 12 and that of the wise woman of Tekoa in 2 Samuel 14, the Bible as canon provides clear mirrors in which we may see the truth about ourselves. David, on hearing Nathan's case, immediately identified with the poor man who had only one sheep; but Nathan said no, David was mirrored by the rich man who had many sheep. And in the mother of the two sons, both the murderer and the murdered, David could see the problems of his own parenthood in regard to Absalom.

The *third* paradigmatic canonical perspective is that we are to theologize on first reading a biblical text. The *fourth* is that we are to moralize only after having theologized. Ask first what the account indicates God was doing; *then* ask what the theocentric reading indicates we can do in and with our lives in the light of it. If we could learn to theologize when reading the ancient texts perhaps we would stop absolutizing the mores of the period from which they derive. Not that the twentieth century has much to say to the Bronze or Iron Ages about mores or ethics. It will probably be known in history, if history there is to be, as the century of massacres, starting with the massacre of the Armenians by the Turks in 1915. In short, our tendencies toward moralizing while reading the biblical texts ring very hollow. Not only that, they produce terrible falsehoods. That circumstance is all the more troubling when one thinks how common it is to moralize on first reading biblical texts.

Lay people can move into reading the Bible as canon if they will follow these simple observations: Read it as paradigms of the struggles of our ancestors in the faith to monotheize, that is, to pursue the Integrity of Reality, in and over against their various polytheistic contexts; and similarly in and over against current polytheistic contexts. The following factors provide a mnemonic device for practical application of the perspectives discussed above: honesty, humility, and humor.

Honesty in this sense means to theologize rather than moralize on first reading a biblical text. Because most folk only moralize in reading the Bible, asking what it says they should do instead of asking what it says God was doing with the likes of us back there, they read it dishonestly. They are reluctant to admit that Abraham and Sarah lied at least twice and at least once each laughed at God.

Humility means, by dynamic analogy, to identify with the not-so-good characters in the texts in order to hear the challenges and the blessings when we do.

Humor means taking God a little more seriously and ourselves just a bit less so each time we read the Bible. God can work with us to weave truth—just as we are. And the promise is that if we believe that and let God in our lives, we will have more programs of obedience and faithfulness occur to us than we could ever hope to fulfill. Obedience comes by faith in what God does and has done more than by our strivings. Remember Paul's great question: in whose works do we have faith, God's or ours (Rom. 9:30—10:4)? If the former, then ours may be effective because they are conceived of and executed in the light of God's. Krister Stendahl, in illustrating the needs of this kind of humor in reading the Bible, points out that no farmer in Palestine ever cast seed on paths, rocky ground or among thorns (Mark 4:3-7); only God would do that!

Finally, theologizing should be done with the view of God that emerges from the canon as a whole, with the full Torah-Christ story in mind. Not with just the Redeemer God of the NT in mind but also with the Creator God of the OT in mind. Not with just the tribal god reflected in some passages in Joshua or Samuel or the Book of Revelation in mind, but with the view of God that emerges from the whole. The Holy Warrior God tempered by the Good Shepherd God (Isa. 40:10–11; 1 Cor. 15:54–57). The God of unfathomable peace tempered by the one who sent Christ for judgment (John 9:39). The God of the Suffering Servant who turns the cheek to the smiters tempered by the one who fought glorious battles to free Hebrew slaves. The God who is both male and female, father and mother to us all. The struggle to love one's enemies while still fighting for what is right is the ongoing dynamic struggle to monotheize: it is a daily commission and charge and will end only when God's *Christus Victor* announces that there is no difference between slave and free, Greek and Jew, male and female. To monotheize now is to rehearse and prepare for that Jubilee.

If clergy and laity in the churches were to discipline their minds to practice a theocentric hermeneutic and learn to theologize on first reading a biblical text, the results could be revolutionary for church and society. This means taking the First and Third Persons, God and Spirit, of the Trinity as seriously as the Second, Christ. To read the Bible on its own terms is to tap a source of power almost beyond reckoning. The word "revival" is not strong enough, in my opinion, to describe the possible effects. I have drawn up *seventeen possible results* of this hermeneutic:

1. It can introduce a truly theocentric perspective in the churches so that God's work of creation in the world and of redemption in Israel, in Christ, and in the early church, can be seen as continuing today.

2. It can reveal for the faithful God's continuing work as Creator of all peoples as well as God's work as Redeemer.

3. It can provide a theological base for learning from current international wisdom as the biblical authors and thinkers did in their day.

4. It may challenge the Christian tendency toward a self-serving reading of the Bible, especially of the NT, with the tendency to feel that Christ somehow domesticated God for us in the incarnation.

5. It can release Christians to honor Christ and worship him as the Second Person of the Godhead, the Son of God, rather than the idol we grasp by our limited ideas of the incarnation.

6. It can seriously challenge Christianity's continuing anti-Semitism and permit us in reading the NT to identify with our just counterparts,

the good religious folk who rejected Christ, and permit us thereby to see our own daily rejections of him.

7. It can, for Christians, put the NT back into the Bible where it belongs and give it the perspective the NT writers themselves had.

8. It can underscore our need to pursue social ethics, and it may put NT personal ethics in a larger canonical perspective.

9. It can help us understand all people in the Bible as humans, God's creatures, hence available for us as mirrors of our own human foibles; it can permit us to see both the splendor and the squalor of all humanity before taking sides on an issue, and perhaps, having done so, it can permit us to love the enemy.

10. It can put NT eschatology in the perspective of God's work as Creator in the first place, as well as re-Creator.

11. It can prepare us for that new creation when there will be truly neither Greek nor Jew, male nor female, slave nor free.

12. It may engender a reading of the whole Bible by the hermeneutic of the freedom of the God of grace so that we could learn how free God's grace really is, even for those we know do not deserve it (like a sheep that gets itself lost, a spoiled younger brother, or those who work only one hour in the cool of the day yet earn as much as the faithful).

13. It can challenge narrow, in-group, denominational readings of the Bible, especially of the NT.

14. It may check the tendency to think God is a Christian (or a Jew, or a Muslim, or a Buddhist) and help the reader remember that God is God.

15. It may help Christians learn that God revealed his Christ as the climax of his own divine story and discourage the tendency to think that *our* Christ revealed God.

16. It may challenge the tendency to read the NT by a self-serving hermeneutic which distorts the doctrines of election and church and permits the thinking that to be "saved" means getting extra rewards rather than serving as eyewitnesses to what God is still doing in the real world today.

17. It can release Christians to evangelize canonically and share the Torah-Christ story, not because we think Christ in the incarnation gave us an exclusive hold on God or out of fear that others are lost—but because out of sheer joy we cannot help but share the vision of the Integrity of Reality this canon affords.

The Bible as canon offers a vision, a way of looking at the world and ourselves in it. To say God is one is to say that Reality has Integrity; and that, all evidence to the contrary notwithstanding, is a matter of faith.

But it provides the believer in that Integrity with the vision to see the incomprehensible yet stubborn desire of that Integrity to touch the lives of all creatures. It releases that believer to see, by that vision, that he or she owns or possesses absolutely nothing in life's brief span but has been appointed a steward of whatever gifts God has entrusted—body, mind, spirit, family, "goods or kindred." To know that "release" is to live a life of Jubilee (Deuteronomy 15; Leviticus 25). It is for the Christian to live in Christ, for Christ is the Christian's Jubilee. The ability to see that truth or reality is the vision that can come from reading the Bible on its own terms.

Appendix

The Triangle

The principal tools of canonical criticism are tradition history and *comparative midrash*, with constant attention to the hermeneutics which caused the authoritative tradition being traced to function in the sociological context where repeated or recited. It is tracing the history of function of a community tradition or a wisdom tradition that puts the current believing communities in touch with their ancestors in the faith who formed and shaped the canon. The perspective is both diachronic and synchronic. The focus is the canonical process.

A very useful tool that has developed out of such work to date is the triangle.[1] It can be superimposed upon the traditioning process at any point along the path of a tradition. Unfortunately, there are not enough clear data at some points along that path to fill in what is needed at the three points of the triangle. But the triangle helps the searcher keep in mind the necessary and essential interrelatedness of the three major factors *always* involved in the canonical process, whether in antiquity while the Bible was being formed and shaped or today when it is called upon to function in modern contexts. As long as there is a canon with a believing community to tradition it, the canonical process is never-ending.

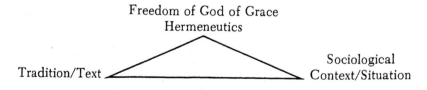

Freedom of God of Grace
Hermeneutics

Tradition/Text

Sociological
Context/Situation

The bottom left angle represents the tradition or text being called upon, recited, or alluded to. This will be the case from the very first repetition in antiquity of a putative tradition taking the initial step

1. James A. Sanders, "Hermeneutics in True and False Prophecy," 21-22; and *God Has A Story Too*, 5-17.

toward canon, all the way to modern lectionaries and the reading of Scripture in worship or study today. Careful discernment of meanings in a text's literary context is essential. All the pertinent tools of biblical criticism are needed here.

The bottom right angle of the triangle represents the historical and sociological context addressed.[2] Context again would exist from the earliest instance of citation or repetition through each layer of repetition right on to modern times, according to what the focus of interest or study may be. Careful discernment of sociological context and the needs of the people addressed is essential. All the pertinent tools of historical criticism are needed here. This is the point at which we attempt careful recovery of the situations of our ancestors in the faith, those believing communities which found value in the traditions and shaped them into canon. It is as important to discern and exegete the sociological context as it is to exegete the text.

The interrelation of these two—text and historical context, down to our own historical context—is the nexus of the Word of God. The same language in two different contexts may mean different things. The Word of God happens or takes place at the nexus of text and context. These very human words our ancestors in the faith have left us may become the Word of God over and over again as our situations and contexts change, and as the Holy Spirit wills.

The top angle represents the hermeneutics by which the tradition functions in the contexts of community present and past. Without clear discernment of the canonical hermeneutics used in the ancient canonical process these very human texts can by other hermeneutics be made to say pretty much whatever the speaker would like them to say. Witness the misreadings of Deuteronomy in exile and many sermons one hears on Sunday night television in this country. Canonical criticism focuses especially upon the unrecorded hermeneutics which lie in and between all the lines of biblical texts. It is the hermeneutics used which determine, in large measure, the meaning of the text. The ears to hear and eyes to see, which one's historical context largely determines, can be opened by the appropriate hermeneutics to hear and see the unexpected and deeper meanings of a text. Canonical criticism, using all the Enlightenment tools of exegesis at each layer of tradition, is especially concerned that resignifications of these canonical texts stay within permissible canonical limits of meaning. The work of determining those limits has begun but is not complete. Concerned scholars must continue to work on this aspect of what remains to be done.

2. Robert Wilson, *Sociological Approaches to the Old Testament* (Philadelphia: Fortress Press, 1984).